A million candles have burned
themselves out. Still I read on.
—Montresor.

CHARRO
Mexican Horseman

The Mexican *charreada,* the father of the American rodeo, in many respects requires more skills and is more exciting. Author James Norman, who has lived in Mexico for many years, introduces you to the *charro,* the Mexican rider who has been called the most skilled in the world. Today amateur horsemen who belong to the Mexican *charro* associations perform in numerous cities nearly every Sunday. The lineage of the Spanish horses that were brought to the New World and spread throughout North and South America is a part of Mr. Norman's fascinating story.

CHARRO
Mexican Horseman

By
James Norman

G.P. Putnam's Sons, New York

To
Michael, Lorian, and Karen Klock

Contents

Acknowledgments

In preparing this book I am indebted to a host of scholars, writers, and horsemen. Although too many archives, old books, and new books were combed through to list in a long bibliography, I should make special mention of the following: José Alvarez del Villar's *La Historia de la Charrería* (Mexico, 1941), the best history of Mexican horsemanship yet written; *El Libro del Charro Mexicano* by Carlos Rincon Gallardo, the Mexican rider's bible; *El Libro de las Charrerías* by Luis Gonzaga Inclan (Mexico, 1886).

I am especially indebted to certain horsemen who let me watch them work or gave me much of their time: Don Alvarez del Villar; Harold Black; General William Fox, USMC, ret.; the members of the Associación de Charros de San Miguel de Allende, and the officers of the Mexican Federación Nacional de Charros.

Among librarians I express thanks to the staff of the Archives of Mexico City and of the Biblioteca Nacional de Mexico. I am also particularly indebted to Dr. Nettie

7

Benson, in charge of the Latin-American collection at the University of Texas Library, and to the staff of the Ohio University Library.

For friendly assistance of many kinds in helping me keep tabs on *charro* events, on Mexican terminology, and in reading manuscripts, I can only make inadequate acknowledgment to Colonel John Johnson of San Miguel de Allende; Dr. Wallace Cameron, department of modern languages at Ohio University; and my wife, Margaret.

1 Where the Action Is

Less than a century ago Americans were a horse people. In the West, where more than 1,000,000 wild mustangs roamed ownerless on the unfenced ranges, men were as much at home in the saddle as Arab nomads. In other sections of the country most families had either carriage or riding horses, and the American boy who could not bridle a horse or cinch a saddle was a rarity.

Today this familiarity with the horse has all but vanished. Cowboys spend more time herding cattle with Jeeps than on horseback, while the few city folks who feel confident in a saddle limit their riding to Sunday morning canters along carefully marked bridlepaths or along well-worn park trails.

In our great cities millions of Americans are born, grow up, and die without ever having seen a real horse. Their idea of horsemanship is gained from movie and television horse operas, in which riders gallop furiously back and forth among lonely buttes, "steering" their foam-flecked mounts with savage jerks of the reins as though they were Mack trucks.

Although skillful riders have almost disappeared in

9

the United States, there are still places in this hemisphere where men ride like centaurs. To the south of us, in Argentina, Venezuela, and Mexico, even though automobiles are rapidly cluttering their highways, the men and women are still horse people. They ride with a flair and daring that often put our professional movie trick riders to shame. Among these countries Mexico, especially, is the place where the action is.

On a Sunday morning when countless Americans perform the ritual of washing and polishing their 200-horsepower Mustangs or Chevrolets before going out for an afternoon pleasure spin, at the same time in Mexico almost as many men and boys are busy saddling their horses for another kind of ride. Instead of taking to bridlepaths or trotting out along a country trail, the Mexicans get together for a lively Sunday morning competition called a *charreada*.

Let us visit the prosperous town of San Miguel de Allende in central Mexico for a glimpse of how many Mexican men, boys, and girls spend their Sundays. The place where they gather together is a kind of corral, called a *lienzo,* usually located at the edge of town. Constructed of stone or brick, plastered over, and whitewashed, it resembles a huge, long-handled frying pan. At one end there is a circular ring which opens into an alleyway about 13 yards wide and 80 yards long. At the butt end of the alley or handle there are smaller pens to hold wild mares, as well as bulls or steers.

While a few men are driving some young bulls into the corrals, at the butt end of the long alleyway a young boy on horseback watches for a signal from a man in the ring. The lad is dressed in the Mexican *charro,* or rider's, outfit: soft brown, high-heeled cowboy boots, tight-fitting suede trousers with decorative braid up the sides, a white shirt, a suede jacket, and a broad-brimmed sombrero.

At a signal from the older man the boy urges his chestnut stallion forward. Although the boy scarcely seems to use his roweled spurs, the horse senses that he is expected to gallop. Horse and rider race up the alleyway, thundering into the ring, speeding across it toward the far wall, where a few spectators are seated in a small grandstand. When it appears as though they will crash into the wall, the horse begins a series of curious braking movements as though he were crouching and sliding. The boy, meanwhile, seems to do nothing to stop his horse. He does not jerk the reins; he does not pull back violently. Nevertheless he remains in control of the horse; his guidance is so subtle and smooth it is as if he and the horse shared a single set of nerves.

When the chestnut finally stands perfectly still, the boy dismounts, remounts, then directs the horse through a series of intricate maneuvers: The horse capers to the right, to the left, pivoting on hind legs that remain fixed to one spot. The boy still does not jerk reins; the dancing capers are directed by a slight pressure of his legs and hands. Finally the rider and horse begin backing across the circular arena into the alleyway. During this exercise, which is done swiftly and smoothly, neither horse nor rider turns his head to see where he is going.

Although the spectators applaud this remarkable performance, the older man now rides to meet the boy and quietly criticizes certain flaws in his horsemanship. This pair, father and son, Jesús and Lucas Godinéz, take their riding seriously, yet neither pretends to be a professional horseman. The father is a local rancher, and the son is a schoolboy who has time to ride only on weekends and vacations.

While they discuss the boy's riding faults, at the butt end of the alleyway a middle-aged man alerts his own horse just as a range-wild steer is released into the runway. As the steer runs parallel to the long wall, the horseman races beside it. The rider gives a curious salute with his right hand; then he slaps the running steer's back several times. Still racing at breakneck speed, the man slides his palm along the steer's spine, catching the beast's tail and letting it slip through his fingers until he has a tight grip on the tufted end. Suddenly the rider raises his right leg and stirrup, hooking it around the animal's tail. With split-second timing he guides his horse slightly to the left and, in the same instant, gives an abrupt pull on the steer's tail, jerking the animal off balance. The steer flips over on his back, four legs straight up, a cloud of dust swirling around him.

When the rider finally halts his horse and picks up his sombrero, which he lost while doing this difficult trick, his companions cheerfully joke about his poor showing.

"Hombre," one of them says, "has your head shrunk that you lose your hat so easily?"

"Man, you should be so careless with money," calls another rider.

The middle-aged horseman nods and grins. He knows that in a formal competition his performance would be penalized twelve points: six for losing his hat, another six for having touched the saddle horn with his left hand as he threw the steer. Still he does not mind making a mistake or two; after all, like the boy Lucas, he is neither a professional horseman nor a rancher. He is the vice-president of a bank.

The banker, still grinning, now turns to watch a wild mare that has been released into the ring and is being driven faster and faster around the circle by other horsemen who shout, *"Andale, andale yegua!"* He also watches an elderly man on foot in the center of the ring. The elderly, blue-eyed, gray-haired man, dressed in the Mexican costume, begins playing out the loop of his stiff lasso. As he whirls the rope, the loop grows larger and larger. It becomes a great spinning O, then its position changes, and it traces marvelous signatures in the air. Although the rope twirler appears indifferent to the mare racing in a wide circle around him, suddenly he flings the loop high into the air and outward toward the sky's infinity as if he intended snaring the billowing clouds rising above the Mexican mountains; then, almost magically the direction of the loop veers, falling swiftly over the haunches of the running mare, where it slips down and catches her two hind legs. As the loop tightens, the gray-haired man pays out rope so that it is neither too taut nor too slack until he brings the horse to a halt without throwing or injuring her.

"Well done, Don Guillermo," shouts one of the riders who had been hazing the mare around the ring. "A nice *peal.*"

The gray-haired man smiles happily. He has been practicing day after day for a number of years to master the throw of the lasso. He appreciates the praise, because he knows that his flourishes with the rope are still far from perfect. For William Fox, who is neither a rancher nor a Mexican, fancy roping is a newly acquired skill. He is a retired U.S. Marine Corps general, a winner of combat air medals, who has settled in Mexico, taking up Mexican horsemanship as a retirement hobby at the age of sixty.

After the men and boys have their morning fill of roping, of tossing steers, and riding wild horses, a group of girls, their ages ranging from twelve to twenty, enter the ring to practice their own spectacular kind of horsemanship. Mounted sidesaddle upon spirited horses, the girls execute complicated patterns, riding back and forth swiftly, weaving in and out, circling and weaving at an ever-increasing tempo. They scarcely seem to use their reins, yet their horses respond with delicate precision. At times they race toward one another, appearing as if they will violently crash, but always they miss one another by bare fractions of an inch. Their riding is like a magnificent ballet performed at breakneck speed on iron-shod animals weighing hundreds of pounds.

Such exciting exercises and many others are indulged in almost every Sunday by thousands of Mexicans in cities and towns throughout the country. The *charreada,* in which they compete with one another and exhibit their equestrian skills, is the ancestor of our Western rodeo; but unlike the present-day North American rodeo, in which riders are generally professional performers striving for prize money, the Mexican horsemen are usually amateurs performing for pure pleasure and sport. The host of Mexican *charros* includes ranchers, businessmen, lawyers, architects, engineers, and schoolboys and girls who like to show what they can do on their superbly trained horses.

The Mexican riders belong to clubs (*charro* associations), numbering about 365 in Mexico, as well as a scattering of *charro* clubs in Illinois, Texas, and California. The membership in these clubs ranges from twenty-five to several hundred riders each. The individual clubs build and maintain the plazas or rings where the horsemen perform. Some members, especially ranchers, have their own private rings where they and their friends can work out.

In order to keep in contact with one another, to arrange interclub competitions, and to hold an annual national competition, the clubs are joined in a national organization, the Federación Nacional de Charros. The club members observe strict rules of courtesy, of dress, and of companionship; many of the rules are based on a 400-year-old tradition of horsemanship. In a sense the *charro* organization might be described as a kind of Mexican Knights of the Round Table—their Camelot is the ranch country.

Although many of the *charros* are city people, they are familiar with ranch work. They often contribute three or four days of their time and their expert help to ranches that are shorthanded at roundup and branding time. Thus the Mexican is never quite as ignorant concerning ranch practices as that professional American rodeo rider who, after having won the bronco busting prize at the Madison Square Garden Rodeo and while traveling by train across Oklahoma, saw a chuck wagon out on the range. Turning to his companion, he asked "What's that gypsy wagon doing way out there?"

In Mexico the *charro* and his horse always play a key role in civic celebrations. They are called upon to lead parades, to welcome the Mexican president and other dignitaries who visit provincial towns, and to keynote all important fiestas.

One of the reasons why riding remains so important in Mexico, in spite of the swift industrialization south of the border, is that the horse is more than just an animal to most Mexicans. The horse is a kind of national figure, a romantic symbol in Mexican history. In what other country, when a horse dies, would the nation's president declare a day of national mourning?

This occurred in Mexico during the 1950's when Arete, a famed cavalry horse which had won numerous international competitions, broke its leg. To determine whether the injured champion could be saved, the Mexican president called upon Latin America's leading bone surgeon to consult with the veterinarians. When it was found that the leg could not be mended and the horse had to be destroyed, a day of national mourning was declared. The Mexican flag flew at half-mast on the National Palace and government buildings throughout the country. Arete was given a formal military burial with a salute of guns equivalent to that rendered a general. The ceremony was broadcast, and millions of people sat by their radios, listening and weeping.

2 Trail of the Ancient Horse

Although horses are noted for their fleetness of foot and their ability to travel great distances—two Argentine ponies were ridden 15,000 miles to Washington, D.C.— the horses of the Americas came to this hemisphere as first-class passengers aboard ships. When Columbus discovered the New World in 1492, there were no horses in the Western Hemisphere.

Millions of years before the historic voyage of Columbus, ancestors of the horse family existed in the Americas. Through twelve long prehistoric periods, beginning shortly after the Age of Reptiles, horselike creatures of various kinds populated both North and South America. Some of these were gigantic specimens measuring 17 hands tall; others were tiny foxlike animals 18 inches tall.

Scientists are not quite agreed upon exactly where the first horse originated. Although the most complete series of fossils covering the long evolution of the horse has been found in America, many naturalists believe that the prehistoric horse first developed in Asia, then gradually populated North America after crossing over the Alaskan land bridges during the Tertiary Period. The progenitor of the horse of the *Equus* tribe may have been an animal with five toes on each foot and teeth like those of a monkey. This early specimen produced many branches, including distant cousins of the horse—the tapir and the rhinoceros.

Perhaps the first horselike animal in the Americas was the fox-size *Eohippus,* which developed a running foot by consolidating its toes; three toes on the hind feet, four on the front. Its teeth also changed, becoming molar-like in order to grind coarse grasses. For millions of years such ancestor-horses changed and developed, adapting to their American and Asian environments. The types called *Mesohippus* and *Merychippus* increased in size and lost their fourth toe. Finally, at the beginning of the Pleistocene Period the true equus evolved its one-toed foot into a running hoof.

For many years experts believed that the horse had disappeared from the American continent long before man appeared upon it. Archaeological evidence now shows that the early horse lived in the Americas at the same time that primitive hunters and horse eaters were crossing the Alaskan land bridge and migrating down as far as Patagonia. Thus the horse and man roamed this hemisphere sometime between 25,000 and 15,000 years ago. Bones of early horses have been found in Peruvian caves along with the bones of early hunters. The horse of that period was not domesticated or ridden.

Countless centuries before these primitive Americans

began to plant seeds and form into civilized communities, the horse vanished. We can only guess at the cause of the extermination of the American equine. Some authorities say that changes in climate deprived the early horse of certain foods and he starved, but this hardly seems possible, because other grass-eating animals—the bison, for example—survived and multiplied. Another explanation is that early hunters killed off or drove horses from their pasturelands. This, too, seems unlikely, considering how large the continent is and how small the population of primitive hunters. The most feasible explanation is that some insect-borne disease destroyed the horse tribe before it could develop an immunity. This theory is supported by the recent discovery of the tsetse fly in Pleistocene deposits in the New World.

Strangely, at about the same time that the horse vanished from the American continent, the horse also retreated from Europe. Horse survivors took refuge on the high Central Asian plateau, from which region, centuries after the last Ice Age, the hardy horse galloped down into Europe and Asia Minor. The trail back to America was a long one.

From Central Asia a kind of dawn horse, the progenitor of modern horses, appeared and divided into two historic types. One was the large, "cold-blooded" animal that lived in swampy or marshy terrain and browsed on the shoots and tender branches of bushes and young trees. The other was the lighter, swifter, "hot-blooded" grazing horse whose natural food was grass. Both horse types went to Europe, but they followed widely separate lanes.

The heavy horse migrated to Northern Europe, where

it found the forests and swamps to be an ideal habitat. When it was finally domesticated by man, it became the parent of such heavy breeds of work and saddle horses as the Belgian, the old English Great or Black Horse, the Shire, the Clydesdale, and the Percheron. These massive, large-footed beasts became the horses of the medieval knights and Crusaders; though they were slow and inefficient in battle, they were capable of carrying tremendously heavy horse armor and a heavily armored knight.

The light horse took a more southern and western route toward Europe. It went first to the hot lands of Asia Minor, where it produced such breed variations as the Arabian horse and the Barb. It adapted perfectly to the warmer climates, to the desert, and to mountain terrains. Also, just as the heavy horse became the war-horse of the armored knights of Europe, the light horse (noted for its endurance, swiftness, and maneuverability) became the war-horse of the lightly clad Arab fighting man. For centuries it was distributed throughout the Mediterranean world by Phoenician traders. Although a few were carried to England, providing an important blood strain for the English Thoroughbred, the majority of the light horses reached Europe through its back door —Spain.

Before entering this gateway to Europe (and to the Americas), the light horse went through certain evolutions. In North Africa a strain of the "hot-blooded" horse was kept and bred by powerful Moorish Caliphs for many centuries. These proud desert horse fanciers maintained a line that was called *asil*, "purebred." The breed, the pure Arabian horse, was set and maintained for so many centuries that even today, more than 1,000 years later, it remains the one horse that exhibits the traits and features of its ancestors. Its blood has been the vital strain in all good riding horses today, be they mustangs, English Thoroughbreds, palominos, Morgans, quarter horses, Hungarian Lippizaners, or Russian Orloffs.

Long before the Middle Ages the Arabian's characteristics were fixed: the marvelous flowing tail, the perfect arch of its neck, the tempered muscles, the bones of almost unbreakable density, the delicate head and nostrils, the alert, intelligent gaze, as well as the remarkable vitality and endurance. It is no wonder that the Arabs, rather than admit that the parent strain of their horse came from the light horse of the Asian plateau, claimed that the first Arabian horse was created out of the wind by God. They say that this equine Adam was a bay or a chestnut; he had a white star on his forehead, a sign of glory and good fortune for its rider.

The second strain of Moorish horse, actually a type rather than a breed, was developed shortly after the time of Christ in the North African Barbary principalities—Tripoli, Fez, Algeria, Morocco, and Tunisia. This horse, called the Barb, was an offshoot of the Arabian. It was sometimes a little larger than the pure Arabian, yet not as large as the heavy horse. Unlike the Arabian, the Barb had a low-set tail in a sloping rump; like the Arabian, it was agile, fast, and noted for its amazing endurance.

Both the Barb and the Arabian were the horses that helped the Moors create one of the greatest empires of the Middle Ages. By the seventh century the Moors had conquered all of North Africa, Egypt, Persia, Syria, and much of Africa. In the year A.D. 710, they entered the back door of Europe, when General Muza and his Berber cavalry landed at Gibraltar and fought northward across Spain. Victory came easily, because Muza's horses, Barbs and Arabians, proved far more maneuverable and superior in cavalry skirmishes than the heavy chargers of the armored Christian knights.

For almost 700 years, until the Moors were driven from the Iberian Peninsula in 1492, Barbs and Arabians became the principal stock horses of Spain. They multiplied especially in middle and southern Spain, where climate and pasture suited them. Soon throughout Europe, where the reputation of Moorish horsemen and their mounts had spread, everyone wanted the famed "Spanish horse"; William the Conqueror, even William Shakespeare, had his eye on the remarkable beast. During these centuries the most famous strain was what the French and English called jennets. The name was derived from the Berber term *"Zenete,"* a powerful North African tribe noted for its horsemanship. In Spain the jennets, raised in Andalusia, were often called Valenzuelas or Guzmanes—the bloodline was said to have been founded by a Barb stallion called Guzmán.

During the long Moorish occupation of Spain there was constant unrest and skirmishes between Moor and Christian. Both sides fought on horseback; the Spaniards, like the Moors, quickly became a race of horsemen. By the time they had driven the Moors back from the Asturias and León in the north to the straits of Gibel Tarik and Gibel Muza, Spaniards had become a well-horsed people who had learned a style of riding which was a preparation for their own conquest-in-the-saddle of the New World, a domain far larger than the Moorish Empire.

When the moment came for horses to board ship and set sail on the long trail back to America (Columbus' second expedition, 1493), the Moorish-Spanish horse had changed somewhat. Although he was called Barb, Arabian, or Spanish, he had acquired a new mixture of blood during his residence in Spain. He had some of the traits of the dun and striped horses Norsemen had brought to Spain long before the arrival of the Moors. He also had characteristics of the Roman horse, which had been bred for six centuries in Spain, and he had some of the blood of the northern horses brought in by the Goths.

In the twenty-five "pilgrim" horses—ten mares and fifteen stallions—which accompanied Columbus across the Atlantic, the hot blood of the light horse dominated. These Spanish-bred animals were tough creatures, admirably suited to the hard work of exploration and conquest. They were short-backed and light-barreled. Their rather lengthy pasterns made them comfortable riding. Their legs were not too long, and being firmly jointed, they were surefooted beasts. Some had the Arabian color characteristics, being unvaryingly solid in color: dark bay, chestnut, gray, nutmeg roan, white with black skin, an occasional black. Among the Arabians there was never a blue or a paint, but among the horses with stronger Barb characteristics there was a rainbow of shades and markings: paints, solid colors, spots, and the blue grullas.

These horses, and others following on their heels, populated the New World islands of Santo Domingo, Cuba, and Jamaica. Although it would be 27 years before they reached the mainland, and it would take another 10 years to establish them in South America, within 300 years these pioneer horses multiplied so rapidly that millions of their offspring went wild, virtually taking over the great plains of North America, the llanos of Venezuela, and the vast pampas of Argentina.

This horse population explosion was particularly amazing, because on March 30, 1520, when the first horse was setting foot on the seared coast of Mexico, Emperor Charles V of the Holy Roman Empire placed a strict embargo on the export of Spanish horses to the New World. From that date onward, with the exception of a few English and Portuguese imports, all the horses of the Americas were the offspring of the Spanish horses brought to the Caribbean Islands during a 27-year period.

What this handful of horses did in the New World is an even more fabulous story. They helped make possible the conquest of two highly developed Indian civilizations with populations numbering almost 20,000,000. They populated a horseless continent. They were mistaken for gods. They wore shoes of pure silver and trappings of gold. But most important, they helped create a 400-year-old tradition of horsemanship that is unique in the world.

3 The Horses of the Conquerors

On March 12, 1519, hundreds of Mexican Indians hid in the bamboo and mangrove thickets along the banks of a tropical river now known as the Grijalva. They warily watched some bearded strangers, who had climbed down from their large sailing ships to smaller boats and were now paddling upstream.

The bearded men were not entirely unknown to the Indians. The year before, another fleet of ships, although not quite as many, had paused at the river mouth while the men had come inland to trade. Nevertheless, the Indians feared the newcomers, having received reports from farther up the coast that they were warlike.

When the boats had come a short distance upstream, at a signal a fleet of Indian canoes filled with warriors pushed out from shore and attacked the invaders. There was a brief, violent battle; then the Indians were forced to withdraw, allowing the bearded men to invade their land and occupy the great central square of their inland city.

Two days later, recovered from the blow, the Indians assembled in even greater numbers to attack the invader.

Beating their war drums and shouting wildly, they charged; showers of Indian arrows and javelins struck the invaders. Although the bearded men resisted furiously, it seemed as though they could not hold out, because there were at least 300 Indian warriors attacking each of the 500 invaders. When victory seemed within the grasp of the Indians, a terrifying sight dismayed them. Fourteen huge, strange monsters suddenly attacked the rear of the Indian companies. The monsters, of course, were Spanish cavalrymen. Startled by this unexpected assault, the terrified Indians fled from the battlefield. Up to this time they had never seen or heard of a horse; they imagined that the horse and its rider were one fierce beast.

This battle, Hernando Cortés' first on the American mainland, reintroduced the horse to the American continent. It also introduced a weapon that would be more decisive for the Spaniards than their few inefficient cannons and even less effective blunderbusses in their daring two-year campaign that toppled the most powerful Indian civilization in the New World.

At first the horses of the Spanish Conquistadors served as a psychological weapon. The Indians believed that the horse and rider were one; perhaps even a powerful god. For example, when Francisco Pizarro rode with his small party down the west coast of South America to begin the conquest of the great Inca Empire in Peru and his party was attacked by an overwhelming number of Indians, the shock value of the horse saved the small party. One of Pizarro's men was knocked off his horse. The man quickly remounted. When the Indians saw this, they were dismayed and withdrew from the encounter, because they imagined that the strange monster, man and horse, was capable of breaking in two and rejoining itself.

Even after the Aztecs and Incas learned that the invaders and their horses were as mortal as they themselves, the Spaniards made sure that their horses continued to instill fear in the hearts of the Indians. Unlike the Arabs, from whom they had learned horsemanship, the Spaniards preferred to ride difficult-to-manage, uncut stallions rather than mares. They convinced the Indians that they bridled their fierce horses to keep them from devouring people. The Indians readily believed that the horses ate their metal bits, that they ran faster than deer and nothing could escape them. Whenever a horse snorted or neighed, the Indians hurriedly fed and watered them to placate their anger.

The first use of this psychological weapon occurred the day following Cortés' victory beside the Grijalva River. Some thirty Indian chieftains came to the Spanish camp to sue for peace. Captain Cortés turned to some of his own men and remarked with a smile, "It seems the Indians are terrified of the horses and think that they alone, with the cannon, make war on them. Bring Juan Sedeño's mare, which foaled the other day on ship, and tie her here. Also bring the stallion of Órtiz, so that he may smell her. Then lead them off separately so the chiefs, when they come, shall not hear the horses neighing until they are standing before me."

When the Indians arrived, one of the Spanish soldiers

brought and tied the stallion, El Arriero, close to where Cortés was standing. Catching the scent of the mare that was hidden in the brush behind the Indians, the stallion began pawing the ground, neighed with excitement, and acted as though he were going to run upon the chieftains. They thought the animal was threatening them. Finally Cortés had his orderly lead the stallion away. He warned the Indians that the horses devoured anyone who opposed the Spaniards. "I have given orders to the horse not to be angry," he said, "as we are all friendly and wish only for peace."

The spirit of Spanish horses, indeed, was enough to frighten any man. Pedro de Heredia, the conqueror of the Colombia coast and founder of Cartagena, had a horse who "was so hot, fierce, and hard to hold he charged into enemy." The horse came out of the skirmish with so many Indian arrows in him that he looked like a porcupine. Heredia managed to save his horse, remove the arrows, and cure him "by bathing him in the sea."

Occasionally Spanish horses took it upon themselves to carry on the conquest of the New World without their riders. The Spanish chronicler Joachin Acosta tells how some Spanish horses, during the Spanish advance on Bogotá, took over some Indian villages:

> Although the natives of those valleys put up some resistance, they were soon broken down and routed by the horses. One night when the Spaniards were camped close to a village, two or three horses that had got loose and galloped through the valley, neighing and jumping, were sufficient to disperse the Indians,

who thought they were as ferocious as the bloodhounds and argued that if the dogs made such havoc in their ranks, how much more terrible the larger animals must be! On the following day the horses were found, having taken possession of the Indian huts.

Although the temper and imposing size of the horses frightened the Indians, the principal value of the horse in the conquest of the Americas was its mobility. A dozen skillful Spanish horsemen, using the light cavalry tactics learned from the Moors, could ride circles around hundreds of Indians on foot. Horses gave the Spaniards the important advantage of being able to scout swiftly and widely, as well as travel long distances.

In spite of their role in the Conquest and in the founding of a great horse culture in this hemisphere, not too much is known about the horses of the Conquistadors. Here and there in the old Spanish chronicles references to the role played by the equine partners can be found. The three principal chroniclers of the horses of the Conquest were: Bernal Díaz del Castillo, a member of Cortés' expeditions; Garcilasco de la Vega, son of an Inca princess and one of Pizarro's soldiers; and Hernando Cortés himself. Of the three, Bernal Díaz was by far the most observant. He carefully listed and described the sixteen horses and their owners who accompanied Cortés in the conquest of Mexico. He wrote:

> I wish to put down here from memory all the horses and mares that accompanied us, and the men who brought them:

Captain Cortés: a vicious chestnut horse which later died at San Juan de Ulua.

Pedro de Alvarado and Hernán López Ávila: a sorrel mare, excellent at both fighting and racing. . . .

Alonzo Hernández Puertocarrero: a silver-gray mare of good speed.

Juan Velázéquez de león: another silver-gray mare, very heavy, called La Rabona [Bobtail], which handled well and was fast.

Cristóbal de Olid: a dark chestnut horse that was pretty good.

Francisco de Montejo and Alonzo de Ávila: a bright-colored sorrel horse, not much good at fighting.

Francisco de Morla: a dark chestnut horse that was swift and handled well.

Juan de Escalante: a light chestnut horse with three white feet, which wasn't any good.

Diego de Ordáz: a barren gray mare that was good enough, but slow.

Gonzalo Dominguez, who was an extremely fine horseman: a dark chestnut horse, very good and a fine runner.

Pedro González de Trujillo: a good chestnut horse —true chestnut—that ran well.

Morón, a citizen of Bayamo: a roan horse with blazed forefeet, which handled well.

Baena, a citizen of Trinidad: a roan horse, almost black, which was good for nothing.

Lares, a very good horseman: an excellent light chestnut horse and fast.

Órtiz, the musician, and Bartolomé Gardía, who once had gold mines: a very good dark horse called El Arriero. This was one of the finest horses that we took on the expedition.

Juan Sedeño, resident of Havana; a chestnut mare that foaled on shipboard.

Few horses were taken on the expedition, for as Díaz wrote; "At that time horses were worth their weight in gold, which is the reason why more horses were not brought." Some of the men, however, acquired horses (shipped from Cuba) during the years of the Conquest. Bernal Díaz speaks of one of Cortés' lieutenants, Gonzalo de Sandoval, who eventually became owner of the best horse of the Conquest, a stallion named Motilla. Sandoval was a bow-legged, exceptional horseman, and Motilla was striking enough for Díaz to say:

He was the best and the fastest horse, and the best bitted, for he turned as well on one side as on the other. [Normally a horse turns best on one side only]. His color was *castañedo* [blood bay] and he had a white star upon his forehead and his near forefoot was white. He was called Motilla. Now, when men talk of horses they say that he is as good or almost as good as Motilla.

Although Bernal Díaz dwelt mostly on the color and temperament of Cortés' horses, giving no thought to their conformation, bloodline, and other characteristics, it is believed that two of the horses were of the noted jennet strain. For the most part, though these horses were small in stature, they must have been quite powerful to carry successfully a semiarmored rider and his equipment—saddlebags, rations, battle-axes, swords, lances, spare horseshoes, and other supplies—across the rugged Mexican highlands.

An unusual kind of natural selection made these horses hardy. During the short period in which horses were shipped in cockle-shell-size vessels from Spain, the least strong were quickly eliminated. It took two months to complete the ocean passage from Spain to Cuba or Santo Domingo and far longer to the River Plate. Aboard ship horses stood on the main deck with little or no shelter. During the deadly calms that delayed the sailing ships, when drinking water and fodder ran short, the sickliest or weakest horses had to be thrown overboard—hence the term "horse lattitudes." When Álvar Núñez Cabeza de Vaca, the appointed governor of Paraguay, landed at Santa Catalina Island in 1540, of the forty horses he had brought with him only fifteen survived. It is estimated that one-third to one-half of all the horses sent from Spain to the New World perished en route; only the hardiest survived.

Those horses that came through the transatlantic ordeal were treated like brothers by the Conquistadors. Cortés, in his letters to the Spanish king, always noted down anything striking that happened to a horse. In his third letter he breaks off an account of a siege to tell what happened to a horse ambushed by the Aztecs. He seemed less interested in the fate of the Spaniard who rode the horse, for he wrote:

> At once she galloped off toward the enemy and they pierced her with arrows. She, when she saw their wickedness, though badly wounded, came back to us. That night she died, and though we felt her death, for the horses and mares were our salvation, our grief was less as she did not die in the power of the enemy as we had feared would be the case.

At times the things that happened to these adventurous horses were strange indeed. The most extraordinary event concerned the stallion, Morzillo, ridden by Cortés on his long expedition from Mexico to Honduras. In 1525, as the expedition reached the margin of Lake Petén-Itzá in Yucatán, Morzillo was crippled by a foot injury, so his master left him in the care of an Indian chieftain who lived on the lake island of Tayasal. Cortés sadly wrote, "The chief promised to take care of him, but I do not know that he will suceed, or what he will do with him."

Cortés never returned for his horse. For 172 years no one knew what had happened to the stallion; then in 1697, during the final conquest of Yucatán, a Spanish military expedition reached Lake Petén-Itzá, where the natives had had no contact with Spaniards since Cortés' visit. As they approached a Maya settlement at the edge of the lake, the Spaniards were startled by the odd behavior of an Indian named Isquin. The moment Isquin saw the Spanish horses he went wild with astonishment.

"Tzimin Chac, Tzimin Chac [Thunder Animal]," he shouted. He dropped to his hands and knees, galloping about on all fours, neighing and imitating the movements of a horse.

Father Bartolomé de Fuensalida and Father Juan de Orbitas, the Maya-speaking chaplains for the expedition, asked the Indian why he was behaving so strangely. Isquin, in turn, wanted to know what the big animals were called. On being told that the Spanish name for them was *caballo,* he forthwith renounced his own name, insisting on being called *caballito,* or little horse.

Through the Indian Isquin, baptized Pedro Caballito, the two missionaries learned that there was a horse named Tzimin Chac on the island of Tayasal. Intrigued by this information, the Franciscan priests went by canoe to the island, where they were welcomed by the Maya-Itzá chieftain Canek. When they inquired about Tzimin Chac, Canek led them to a temple where he proudly showed them the large stone idol which his people worshiped. The carved stone figure on the altar was that of a horse seated on his hindquarters, his front legs thrust stiffly forward—a most peculiar pose for a horse. It was the statue of Cortés stallion.

Villaguiterre, the expedition's historian, has explained what happened to Morzillo. Awed by the great horse which had been left in their care, the Indians, believing he was a reasoning animal (*"entiendo que era animal de razon"*), housed Morzillo in one of their temples and fed him what they thought were proper delicacies: fish, deer meat, tropical fruit, and roast duck. The unusual diet soon killed the stallion. Terrified by what had happened, the Indians buried Morzillo; then they made a life-size statue of him, which was placed in the temple and became the chief deity of the islanders.

The speed at which the Spanish horse and his rider got around the Americas is incredible. In less than forty years, 1520 to 1560, they penetrated, conquered, and began to settle across the continental spread of North and South America. With each new expedition additional horses were brought to the horseless land.

Diago de Ordáz, one of Cortés' lieutenants, headed southward to conquer all the country from El Cabo de las Velas (Venezuela) down to the north bank of the Amazon. He took with him 50 head of horses from the royal ranch at Jamaica.

Hernando de Soto, one of Pizarro's greatest horsemen, turned from the conquest of Peru, leading a disastrous three-year expedition across what is now Florida, Georgia, Alabama, and the Carolinas to the Mississippi River. Of the 600 men and 250 horses who set out in 1539, few of the men and no horses returned to civilization. De Soto himself died and was buried along the Mississippi.

At almost the same time (1540) Francisco Vásquez de Coronado led an even larger expedition into the region of New Mexico. He took with him some 1,500 horses, mules, and donkeys.

During all these expeditions horses were killed in battle, some ran away, others were stolen by Indians. De Soto lost all his horses. Coronado suffered heavy horse and mule losses. The Pedro de Mendoza expedition gave up the 1541 attempt to settle Buenos Aires, losing or destroying the expedition's seven remaining horses before abandoning the area. Such losses did not indicate that the Spaniards were careless with horseflesh. During the years of the Conquest an ordinary horse was worth a fortune.

Immediately after the conquest of the Inca Empire, horses were being sold in Peru for 6,000 gold pesos— the price of a Cadillac. Some twenty years later the new governor of Paraguay, Don Domingo Martónez de Irala, still had to pay 4,000 gold crowns for "a black horse with a white blaze on his forehead, and a white stocking on his near foot."

Today romantic-minded, uninformed people claim that the runaway or captured horses of the Conquistadors gave birth to the great wild herds what spread over the Americas. This is hardly likely because the horse was too expensive and too important to lose. During the Conquest every man knew that his life might depend on a horse. Bernal Díaz wrote, "In the unrelenting fight of one against thousands, the horses were our fortresses, our only hope of survival." Pedro de Casteñeda de Nagera, who accompanied Coronado, summed it up in another way, saying, "Horses are the most necessary things in the new country because they frighten the enemy most, and after God, to them belongs the victory."

A few of the Conquistadors' horses may have run wild, but these served to breed more legends than they did horses. It is appropriate that one of Cortés' horses should have started the ball rolling. Mexican folklore has it that the first horse to run wild in the Americas was the colt that had foaled on shipboard just before Cortés' first battle at the Grijalva River. When the Spaniards began their hazardous march from the coast to the high Mexican heartland, the colt was separated from its mother and lost. After the fall of the Aztec Empire, Spaniards and Indians reported that this pony had been seen running wild with a herd of deer on the lower slopes of the majestic, snow-capped Mount Orizaba. A Spanish rancher claimed he captured the young horse and corraled it with his own animals. It refused to be tamed and soon escaped, rejoining the deer. Even today Mexicans say that the lost colt is sometimes seen in the wild country, and anyone who sees it will have good luck. Naturally the color of the colt was white. The legend was the first of many such tales about marvelous, wild white mustangs.

In his delightful book *The Mustangs,* J. Frank Dobie discounts the Adam and Eve role of such wild horses with gentle irony. He wrote:

> . . . The pretty legend has an escaped De Soto mare sniffing her way west from somewhere along the Mississippi until, far out on the plains, an eastward-sniffing stallion escaped from Coronado's *caballada* scents her. Oh, joy! and there the multiplication of mustangs begins. If another fable had placed Adam in Asia and Eve in Africa, the chances of mating would have been about as high.

The spectacular growth of the great wild horse herds in North and South America was the result of another facet in the character of the Spanish horses of the conquerors. The horses brought to the New World by Cortés and other adventurers were not merely war-horses. They had been shipped from Spain to the islands for purposes of colonization. Most of them had been trained as cow horses. In Spain the techniques of ranching—herding cattle on horseback, roundups, and branding—had already been developed by 1492. Arriving in the Americas, the Spanish horse never forgot its trade. On the long expeditions—Cortés through Mexico and Honduras, Pizarro to Peru, Coronado to the Northwest—the horses of the Conquistadors always worked livestock. The rations for the explorers, beef-on-the-hoof, was driven ahead.

For the answer to how the horse multiplied in the Americas and how they contributed to a distinct school of horsemanship, we must turn to the story of Mexican ranching.

4 Caballero into Cowboy

The 700-year Moslem occupation of Spain turned the Spaniards into expert cavalrymen; the 300-year Spanish domination of the New World turned the colonists into ranchers. Ranching laid the foundation and traditions for a vivid style of riding that is uniquely American. It also created a horse culture later epitomized by the Texan expression "A man on foot is no man at all; a man is no better than his horse."

While the conquest of the new lands was still in progress, official steps were taken to make every man a horseman. In Mexico Cortés issued an order stating that Spaniards must be mounted, and they should develop equestrian skills. In 1526, when it was noted that many of the colonists preferred riding less expensive, easier-going mules, the authorities issued an edict stating that no one could own a mule unless he also owned a horse. Two years later the king's representatives in Mexico and other colonies further tightened the law: Able-bodied men were absolutely prohibited aboard mules; only the clergy and persons less than fourteen years of age or over seventy were exempted. Other laws discouraged the raising of mules and encouraged the breeding of horses. The penalties for breaking these laws were severe.

These regulations applied only to Spaniards and colonists of direct Spanish descent. The conquered people, the defeated Aztecs, Incas, and other Indian nations, were not allowed to ride anything. They were condemned to be pedestrians. Knowing that the horse gave them an enormous advantage over the Indians, the Spaniards meant to keep that valuable animal out of their hands. The Second Audiencia, a governing committee representing the king in Mexico, imposed a penalty of death on any colonist who gave, sold, or lent horses and mares to the Indians.

Although such laws remained on the books for almost 300 years, it was impossible to enforce them. At the very beginning the Spanish leaders instituted exceptions. When an Indian rebellion in western Mexico seriously threatened the colonists during 1541, Don Antonio de Mendoza, the first viceroy, put friendly Aztec chieftains on horseback so they could war against the insurgent Indians. The first two Indian leaders equipped with horses were Nicolás Montañez, chief in the Tula-Jilotepec region, and Fernando de Tapia, chieftain of the Otomó Indians. Montañez left a written record, saying:

> The Viceroy sent me arms, thirty guns and one hundred horses. I mounted my white horse called Valona, which had a white moon on his face, and led my army and subdued the barbarian Chichimecas.

Nor were the Indian nobles, friends of the Spaniards,

the only natives to become horsemen. On the large cattle and horse ranches, which mushroomed in the colonies, the herdsmen, all Indians, frequently rode horses in the course of their work. They were the first *vaqueros,* or cowboys, of the New World.

These first "horse" Indians rode bareback, because another colonial law expressly prohibited them from using the saddle or the bit. The English traveler Henry Hawks, who spent five years in New Spain, wrote:

> The Spaniards held the Indians in great subjugation, forbidding them to have in their houses swords, daggers, knives with points, and forbidding the use of all kinds of arms. They also forbad the Indians to mount horse or mule in any kind of saddle.

To make certain that the Spanish horseman was dominant, a system of *alardes* (reviews) was instituted in the colonies. These horseback drills were similar to the militia drills conducted years later by the North American colonists. The first of these impressive reviews held on New World soil occurred April 19, 1519, when Cortés debarked his expedition on the beach at Veracruz. To impress the Indians who were watching, he immediately ordered a parade of all his men and horses. Bernal Díaz wrote that the review included "458 soldiers in eleven companies, 109 sailors, ten cavalrymen and their mounts."

As towns and settlements sprouted across the land after the Conquest, *alardes* were held regularly in each community; all able-bodied men were required to assemble, completely armed and mounted, once every four months. During these reviews the horsemen performed formation maneuvers to impress the conquered people. Later, as the threat of Indian uprisings vanished, these equestrian assemblies changed in character, evolving into parades or *regocijos* (pleasure parades). At these festive events the horsemen wore handsomely decorated costumes; they exhibited their prize horses, their beautifully decorated saddles, and silver embellished bridles. Some horses even wore silver shoes, although at first this was not a sign of ostentation—there was more silver than iron available.

In Latin America it is customary, when a soldier rises to a generalship or a politician scales the political ladder, that he acquire a large ranch. This practical tradition began with the Conquistadors. The Pizarro brothers in Peru, and Cortés and his lieutenants in Mexico staked out horse ranches long before the Indians were completely subdued. During his term of office between 1535 and 1550, the first viceroy of New Spain acquired twelve horse and cattle haciendas in the region around Mexico City.

By 1530, less than eight years after the fall of the Aztec capital, Tenochtitlán, fourteen horse-breeding ranches were registered by the Mexico City authorities. Brand marks on horses and cattle were already being recorded. The tradition of branding horses anywhere on the right-hand side was common in Spain and was carried to the Americas. The reason behind the right-side marking was that in a corral, horses were usually run from the right to the left; thus they were easier to identify. In time this changed; now, normally, an animal is branded on the left rear hip. In the Americas the tendency also developed to hide or reduce the size of the disfiguring brand marks; they were placed on the jaw, under the mane, or, as in Argentina, beneath the saddle blanket.

A remarkable recording of the brand marks on Cortés' original seventeen horses was made by the Mexican Indians in a pictographic codex called the *Lienzo de Tlaxcala*. Tlaxcalan Indian artists carefully sketched the arrival of the Spaniards in their city, recording in their drawings the brand marks on each of the horses (right side), as well as every detail of the Spanish saddles, the bridles, and even the riding style of the conquerors.

Before the end of the sixteenth century, ranching had spread like wildfire across Mexico, Honduras, Nicaragua, Venezuela, Peru, and Argentina. Along with silver and gold mining, it became one of the most important industries in the New World. The growth of the ranches was often closely allied with the mining industry: beef was needed to sustain the miners; hides furnished the raw material for the heavy sacks used for carrying ore from the mines; leather was used for clothing and frequently for household furnishings.

The need for hides was so important that some of the conquerors took up buffalo (bison) hunting. One adventurer, Juan de Oñate, thought he could make a fortune in buffalo hides in New Mexico. He sent his lieutenant, Vicente Zaldívar, out to build a corral for 100,000 head of buffalo. Zaldívar built the corral near the Pecos River, then tried to drive the bison into it. For three days he and his men tried every cattleman's trick to corral the first herd of 300 animals. The results were disastrous: three of Zaldívar's horse were killed, 40 horses were injured; not a buffalo was captured. Zaldívar disgustedly gave up the project, saying, "It was impossible to stop them because they are terribly obstinate cattle and courageous beyond exaggeration."

Ranching developed so rapidly after the Conquest that it threatened the livelihood of the Indians who, until the coming of the Spaniards, had no domestic animals except dogs, turkeys, and, in Peru, llamas. The grazing animals of the Spaniards required extensive lands; thus in order to protect the Indian farmlands, the Spanish crown ordered cattle, horses, and sheep ranches to move farther and farther from the centers of population. The move to the uninhabited, vast range country made the horse the kingpin of cattle raising.

The horse population in the Americas kept pace with, and in fact outstripped, the growing cattle industry. Within a century after the Conquest horses settled and thrived in the New World as they had nowhere else. The great pampas of Argentina, the llanos of Venezuela, the broad prairies of northern Mexico perfectly suited the horse. The Spanish horse, essentially domesticated and stable-bred in the Old World, quickly acclimatized to a newer and freer life.

The Argentine pampas, where there was no extreme cold, or heat, or predatory animals, became a horse paradise. Forty years after Pedro de Mendoza had been forced to abandon the first colony in the Buenos Aires region, the area, according to the Spanish observer Don Juan Garay, was full of wild horses. During one period covering 100 years the pampas actually supported more feral horses than North America had at any one time. The Argentine wild horse, called a *baguale,* became such a nuisance it almost ruined the cattle industry.

While making a long horseback journey across the pampas in 1744, the English Jesuit Thomas Falkner said that he had seen *baguales* in such numbers that:

> . . . during a fortnight they continually surrounded me. Sometimes they passed by, in thick troops, on full speed, for two or three hours together, during which time it was with great difficulty that I and the four Indians who accompanied me preserved ourselves from being run over and trampled to pieces by them.

Another traveler, the naturalist Azara, wrote, "I saw herds of *baguales* amounting, without exaggeration, to ten thousand."

Peru, where Pizarro toppled the Inca Empire, soon became South America's horse-breeding center. Peruvian breeders in the Charcas region supplied the southern continent, including Argentina, wtih most of its horses. It was from the Charcas region that Don Pedro de Valdiva, in 1541, introduced the first horse to Chile. In Central America, Nueva Valladolid (Honduras) became an equally important stock-raising center.

In Mexico and North America the spreading of cattle and horse ranches and the growth of the great mustang herds were largely due to missionaries and a few second-generation Spanish colonizers. In 1562 Francisco de Ibarra, a colonizer, brought horses to Nueva Vizcaya (the present-day Mexican states of Sonora, Durango, Sinaloa, and Chihuahua), but more than anyone, an Italian-born Jesuit priest carried the horse culture to the north.

Father Eusebio Kino, a noted mathematician and map maker, who had had no youthful experience with horses, arrived in Mexico in 1661. He was sent to explore the west coast of Mexico and Lower California, then to establish missions in the Pimeria Alta territory (the unexplored region of northern Sonora and southern Arizona). Father Kino proved to be both a great missionary and horseman; he preached to thousands of Indians, taught them to plant new crops and raise cattle; he founded twenty-four missions, and to supervise them, he made forty horseback trips, each 1,000 to 3,000 miles in distance. On some of these rides he went alone; on others he was accompanied by Indians he had taught to ride.

The great wild horse herds were the products of these northern haciendas and mission ranches. From time to time small numbers of horses were cut out or stampeded from the mounts of Spanish expeditions. More often an Indian *vaquero* at a mission ranch, homesick and tiring of Christian civilization, would steal away on a mission horse. Then, in 1680, during the great Pueblo revolts, thousands of horses and cattle were let loose to spread across the American Southwest as a result of the Indian raids on the missions.

In California, which was horsed later than any other area, something in the air and the grass made horses thrive better than anywhere else. Not long after Gaspar de Portolá's expedition introduced the first 39 horses to the golden shore, horses were breeding like the rabbits in Australia. California horses, like Father Kino's horses, were prolific. It was the custom among New World ranchers to let their stallions and bulls go uncut; the potency of these animals on the virgin ranges was an enormous factor in stocking the Americas. As happened in Argentina during the early nineteenth century, where 500,000 wild horses had to be slaughtered annually to preserve graze land for cattle, in California thousands of wild horses were driven off the cliffs at Santa Barbara into the sea, while other thousands were destroyed in corrals.

On the Great Plains, especially in Texas, the wild-horse population reached well over 1,000,000 head. John R. Bartlett, a Texas rancher, once described the tremendous herds, saying, "The prairie near the horizon seemed to be moving, with long undulations, like the waves of an ocean. . . . The whole prairie was alive with mustangs."

Young Lieutenant Ulysses S. Grant, considered to have been the finest horseman to come out of West Point in the 1840's, described a similar wild-horse herd near the Nueces River in Texas:

It was the very band from which the horse I was riding had been captured but a few weeks before. . . . As far as the eye could reach to our right, the herd extended. To the left, it extended equally. There was no estimating the animals in it; I have an idea that they could all have been corralled in the State of Rhode Island, or Delaware, at one time. If they had been, they would have been so thick that the pasturage would have given out the first day.

A year later in the same region Thomas Dwyer, an Irish lawyer turned horse rancher, looked at a Texas mustang herd and said:

Thousands and tens of thousands of wild horses running in immense herds all over the western country, as far as the eye or telescope could sweep the horizon. The whole country seemed to be running!

As ranchers and missions moved northward, the very thing the early Spanish colonizers feared occurred swiftly —the Indian was horsed. This had already happened in South America where, shortly after the introduction of the horse in Argentina, the Patagonian Indians were so well mounted they hardly stirred a step on foot. In North America the Indians, pedestrians for countless centuries and unable to trap the fleet-footed wild horses beginning to populate the region, took their first horses from the missions. Once mounted, they were able to secure remounts from the wild mustang herds.

Although this book deals with the style of horsemanship that originated in Morocco and Spain and evolved in Mexico, a word should be said about the Indian contribution to it, even though it is minor. Once mounted, the northern Indian developed remarkable ways with horses. Along the Río Grande early settlers used to say:

A white man will ride a mustang until it is played out; a Mexican will take over the animal and ride it another twenty-four hours until he thinks the horse is played out; then a Comanche will mount it and ride it to where he is going.

The Comanches and Kiowas were the most spectacular horsemen. They could drop to one side of a running horse, exposing only the sole of a moccasin to the enemy, and shoot arrows from beneath the animal's neck. On buffalo hunts they had so trained their mounts that the horses automatically swerved to one side at the twang of a bowstring so as to avoid the falling bison. The Comanche's skill at getting the most out of a horse is vividly illustrated in the story of a famous horse race staged by U.S. cavalrymen and some Comanche Indians at Fort Chadbourne on the Texas frontier.

The Comanche chieftain had agreed to race his fastest mustang against anything the Americans had, and this included a fine Thoroughbred Kentucky mare. When the cavalry officers saw the Indian pony, "a miserable sheep of a pony with legs like a churn," they withdrew their Thoroughbred and ran one of their regular cavalry mounts. In this race and in a second race against another cavalry horse, the churn-legged mustang was victorious.

Irritated, the officers proposed a third race in which they would run the Thoroughbred. Confident that they would not lose this time, they bet rather heavily with the gathered Comanches. For the third time that day the "miserable sheep of an Indian pony" appeared at the starting line. To add insult to lost wagers, during this final race the Indian pony not only shot into the lead, but during the last leg of the race the Indian rider reversed himself on his ragged mustang, sitting face toward tail. According to Colonel Richard Dodge, the post commander, the Indian was "making hideous grimaces and beckoning our man to catch up."

Although the sedentary Indians of central Mexico never were spectacular horsemen like their northern cousins, they contributed to the development of the Mexican horseman and horsemanship. In Mexico, especially on the great landed estates, Indians and Spaniards intermarried, creating a caste. This caste, the *mestizo,* that is to say, people of mixed blood—now the bulk of the Mexican population—were for centuries the backbone of the ranching industry. They were the men who worked as foremen and cowhands on great haciendas or who owned and ran their own small ranches; they were the men who contributed most, not only in the development of ranching techniques, but in creating a style of riding and a method of training horses that is distinct from the Spanish equestrianism or riding style of the *caballero.*

5 The Mexican Way of Riding

It is a surprise that in a country like Mexico, where a distinctive style of horsemanship has been developed, no one has organized an institution to collect the knowledge of its riders and to establish a school of equestrianism similar to those found in European countries. According to Don José Alvarez de Villar, a historian of Mexican equestrian history, "A Mexican school does exist—but it exists implicitly." The Mexican school or Mexican system of horsemanship did not develop by accident. To quote a Mexican proverb, "Horses and horsemen are not born; they are made." In Mexico the horse and horsemanship were shaped by Mexican history.

The origin of the peculiarly Mexican way of riding goes back to the Spanish school called *jineta*. At the time of the Conquest Spanish gentlemen practiced two styles of riding: *a la brida* and *a la jineta*. The first (*a la brida*) was an ancient type of horsemanship developed by the medieval European knights. The completely armored, top-heavy warrior rode upon a Bur saddle which had a well-

51

padded seat, a low cantle, and wings that pressed the rider's knees against it, presumably so he wouldn't lose his balance and topple to the ground. The horseman sat absolutely erect, his legs thrust straight down as though he were standing in the long stirrups. The position was dictated by the excessive weight of the rider's armor. The reins were held low, the horse's head being jerked to the left or right to turn him. Altogether this made for a stiff, awkward style of riding.

The *a la jineta* school of riding was a Moslem gift to Spain. The name, as we know, was derived from the Zenete tribe of Berber horsemen. A man who rode *a la jineta* used a light saddle placed well up on the withers of the horse. The stirrups were so short that the rider seemed to be kneeling upon his mount. The rider rode with a high hand, that is to say, the short reins were held high because the horse was "bitted" on the neck; he was turned by the pressure of the reins on the neck rather than being guided by pulling at the corners of the mouth in the European fashion.

It is curious that the *a la brida* school of riding was still practiced in Spain when the New World was discovered, because the Moslem system had already proven itself far superior. The *a la jineta* warrior, unencumbered by heavy armor, riding a swifter, more agile horse that responded instantly to his body movements and a touch of the reins, was like a skilled lightweight fighter dancing around a clumsy heavyweight. Perhaps the old style persisted simply because of tradition. In Spain the highest praise a man could receive was to be called a cavalier who rode well in both saddles—*ser jinete in ambas sillas.* When he died, his family inscribed the fact that he rode both ways on his tombstone. The medieval traditions of chivalry, of romance, and of knighthood did not pass away easily. It took the comicotragic knight Don Quixote and his realistic partner, Sancho Panza, to ridicule the old traditions to death. Sancho knew what was best; when he was made governor of the fictional principality of Baratania, he received the honor mounted on a mule, *a la jineta.*

Like Sancho Panza, the Spaniards who came to the New World were practical men. Although they rode the Moslem way—the Inca Garcilasco de la Vega said, "My country was conquered *a la jineta*"—they brought with them a slightly modified Moorish saddle, and they lengthened the stirrups somewhat for the longer difficult journeys they had to make. They also developed other riding habits useful in the New World. They never rode with the reins tied, because if they were dismounted in battle, the free reins, falling to the ground, were easier to catch, and there was less chance of their mounts running away. They also learned to tie a horse properly, so the knot neither ran hard nor slipped. They learned to mount in one motion, never standing in the stirrup with one leg posed stiffly in the air after the style of riding schools.

During the first years of Spanish domination in the Americas gentlemen riders maintained the *a la jineta* forms of horsemanship especially for their parades, their horse drills, and in certain military-type games, which will be described later. However, as soon as haciendas and ranches became both the backbone of the economy and the center of social life outside large cities, a purely American style of horsemanship developed according to the needs and tastes of each region—Mexico, Venezuela, Peru, and Argentina.

Certain local needs forced New World horsemen to abandon the strictly Spanish mode of horsemanship and to develop their own national forms. On ranches, for example, the Mexican rider worked out a style of mounting his horse that was quite different from the *a la brida* or *a la jineta,* where horses were either heavy and slow—the armored knight being hoisted on a stationary horse—or docile, as the Arabian mare. Drawing their horses from the range, often from wild mustang herds, the Mexican rider learned to stand in front of the near shoulder of his horse, facing toward the tail; with his right hand he twisted the stirrup halfway around, holding it in position; meanwhile, his left hand threw the reins over the animal's head and at the same instant caught the saddle horn. The instant his foot went into the stirrup the horse moved forward, actually snapping the rider into the saddle. In this style of mounting, the right rein was held shorter than the left, tending to swing the starting horse under the rider rather than away from him. Some athletic cowmen and *charros,* scorning the stirrup, swung into the saddle with a flying start or mount.

Even more than mounting, the seat or riding position of the horseman has been the subject of vehement argument among Mexican riders ever since colonial days. How a man sits his horse depends on numerous things: the shape of the saddle, where it is placed on the horse, the length of the stirrups, the balance and rhythm of the rider. A sixteenth-century equestrian writer, Bernardo de Vargas Machuca, suggested in riddle form what the proper length of the stirrup should be, saying, "The stirrup should be more short than long for graceful riding, and in truth more long than short."

He simply meant there should be a compromise between the long, straight-legged stirrup, which set the rider as dead weight upon a horse, and the extremely short *a la jineta,* jockeylike length that placed the rider too far forward of the horse's center of balance. A stirrup that bends the leg slightly, giving the rider a slightly forward seat, helps him grip the horse's barrel in a natural manner. If the saddle seat is shaped properly, the horseman sits erect, yet without stiffness. He rides with resilience, is balanced in all gaits, and he is able to shift his live weight with the changing movements of his horse.

The *charro* style of riding, evolved over centuries, eliminates the stiff posturing of most equestrian schools. Instead the rider exhibits exceptional ease, balance, and rhythm. Even if he falls asleep while riding, his rhythm will change with every change of the horse's pace, and he becomes, in a manner of speaking, an extension of the flesh and muscles and nerves of his mount. Like the Moslem and Spanish rider, the *charro* rides with a high hand, bitting the horse on the neck as well as guiding him with deft body movements and signals.

Much of the unique riding style of the Mexican *charro* is dependent on his methods of gentling and training his

mount. Like the Arabs, Mexican *charros* have tradition-
ally believed that a horse should spend its first four or five
years under the open skies, hardening itself to weather,
terrain, and even hunger. During this period the horse
reaches a physical and mental state called *cerrado* (mature). By its fifth or sixth year the horse is ready to be
trained. At four years a horse can be trained, but it must
be done carefully, never overworking the youngster.

This is, indeed, a contrast to the present-day American
practice of stuffing a colt with grain as soon as he is
weaned and then, as John Richard Young, the notable
horse trainer, says, "riding him, often in competition as a
two-year-old."

When the *charro* thinks his horse is mature, the animal
is "gentled" rather than broken. Since range-bred horses,
unlike the stable horses of Europe, have a tendency to
buck and shy, the gentling process is a slow, difficult one.
Thanks to our Wild West novels and movies, most of us
have the notion that the only way to gentle a horse is to
dominate him by sheer guts and force.

Bronco "busting" of this sort was not the exclusive tal-
ent of North American cowpokes. Hundreds of years ago
in Argentina the celebrated gaucho Rosas would hang
from the crossbar above a corral gate; when the gate was
flung open and a herd of wild horses raced out, he fell
astride the *baguale* he had previously spotted for its
strength and wildness. Without bridle or saddle he stuck
to the horse, eventually riding it back to the corral.

The twelve-dollar wild mustang Ulysses S. Grant
bought in Texas was treated in the same way. Grant had

his friends blindfold the horse while it was fitted with a Spanish saddle and bridle. According to Grant's companion, the future Confederate General James Longstreet:

> When Grant was firmly in the saddle he threw off the blindfold. The wild animal stood trembling for a moment, then launched into a series of leaps and bucks and twists while the spectacle brought soldiers running from all directions. Finally, at the instant when the stallion's will showed the first hint of weakening, Grant loosed the reins, struck home with his spurs, and the two, horse and man, held together like the famous centaur, streaked across the plain and disappeared in the spiny thickets of chaparral. Three hours passed, and I wondered if I would ever see Grant again. Then he came in, the stallion's head down, the skin dripping with sweat.

Professional broncobusters were even harder on horses. Their technique was to intimidate a horse, break his spirit, and physically exhaust him. They would rope a wild horse and violently throw him to the ground. Then they would haze and beat him with a stick or quirt until he seemed chastened. Then they would saddle and mount him, quirting and roweling him without mercy.

The *charro*'s method of gentling a horse is far different, because he doesn't "break" a horse to sell him, he "gentles" him in order to train him. Patience is the key. The *charro*'s method begins with lessons learned from Indians who became the first cowboys after the Spanish Conquest.

A description of this method was given by Father Pedro Barrientos, a Spanish missionary and accomplished horseman who came to the Americas in 1544. Working with the Indians of Guatemala, Father Barrientos said that when they set out to gentle a horse, they first tied the animal securely to a tree. One of the Indians would climb the tree and, hanging from the branches, would lower himself until his feet just touched the horse's back. The man continually raised and lowered himself until the horse grew accustomed to his touch, then his weight. The next step, still holding to the branches, was to lower himself until he was astride the horse. This was sometimes repeated for days until the animal accepted the rider.

Mexican Indians, before attempting to mount a range horse, spent days merely caressing and touching the horse, running hands over his face, head, chest, back, legs, and haunches. At times they breathed into the animal's nostrils. J. Frank Dobie, speaking of this latter technique, said:

> There may be something to it. No wild animal feels acquainted with anything strange until it has smelled it. . . . I have seen *vaqueros* do this, not only to mustangs, but to wild cows and calves.

The *charro* works similarly. He ropes a spirited horse with sufficient skill so the animal is not injured. A hackamore is gradually introduced. During all this time the *charro* talks gently to the animal, rubbing and touching him until the horse becomes calm. By means of the hackamore the animal is walked about, usually in a ring or area where no other animals or people can become a distraction. Such training may take days, and only when the hackamore can be put on and removed without opposition is the horse ready for the next step, cavesson training.

The cavesson (*cabezón*) is a simple leather halter that adjusts snugly to the horse's head. It has a metal ring on each side of the noseband so that false reins can be attached and run back to the saddle; a metal ring is also fixed to the front of the noseband. A strong, light, long line is attached to the ring and is used for leading the horse. The cavesson permits the animal to be trained in various paces, turns, and stops before the bit is introduced.

Most expert *charros* introduce the saddle and rider before bitting a horse. Acquainting a horse to the saddle is done with equal care and patience. The animal is first accustomed to the feel of the saddle blanket, then the saddle. He is run through his various paces with the saddle cinched and the stirrups tied down but without a rider.

When the animal has completely accepted the saddle, the mounting lessons are begun. While calmly reassuring the horse, the trainer repeatedly places his weight in the stirrup, rising upon it and dropping to the ground. When the animal is used to this, the trainer finally throws his right leg, without bending it, over the animal's croup, then gently eases himself into the saddle. The horse, carrying his rider, is still led through his paces by the long line and cavesson.

The last step is to fit the horse with bridle and bit. The

best bit is a soft one having no chains, barbs, or wire snaffles.

Such time-consuming "gentling" pays off. The horse has developed confidence in his trainer and rider; the rider has begun to learn the talents, limitations, and quirks of his mount. Both are now ready for the equally slow but fascinating work of training the animal for *charro*-style exercises. The *charro* spends a minimum of three hours a day exercising and caring for his horse, as well as training the animal to respond to hand and leg signals, to work with cattle, to work with the lasso, and to be a skilled partner in tailing bulls.

The *charro* school of riding, so uniquely Mexican, combines the drama and flamboyance of the Spaniard and the fantasy and color of the Mexican Indian. Its skills, its colorful costumes, its flourishes, and its gestures are a summation of Mexican history and a reflection of the Mexican personality.

6 The Charro's Horse

Like the *charro's* style of riding, the *charro's* horse has changed over the centuries—and is still changing.

The original mount was the Spanish horse of Barb and Arabian blood. In the Americas these stallions and mares produced a variety of types: cavalry mounts, carriage horses, cow horses, plow plugs, packhorses, mustangs, and *baguales.* The color range was even greater: browns, bays, blacks, chestnuts, piebalds, roans, grays, duns, clay-banks, skewbalds, calicoes, cream-colored with black points; or their Spanish names: *pintos, panagarés, lo-bunos, grullas, tordillos, melados, pampas, picazos, gate-ados, zaunos, roanos, overos, doradillos, barrosos,* and *bayos.*

The rainbow spectrum was more common to the North American continent, and it seemed to have stopped at the Amazon River. The South American horses, even the wild *baguales,* seldom exhibited the variety of colors marking the horses of the North. Among the Paraguay and Argentine *baguales* the most common shadings were darkish browns, bays, and chestnuts. Today a greater variety of colors can be found in South America because of the import of Friesland horses into Brazil by the Dutch.

The conformations and the nature of these horses vary considerably. Forced to rely on themselves for protection in the New World, the offspring of the original Spanish horses developed marked charactristics not found in their Iberian ancestors. Let loose on the open range, having to cope with unaccustomed enemies such as pumas, coyotes, and wildcats, the horse had to react more swiftly than its European cousins. His hearing became sharper, his eyesight more acute. According to Darwin's theory of natural selection the horses which possessed traits that made them adaptable to life in the New World survived while those that did not died off.

The lines of the New World horse changed with each region. In Argentina the *criollo,* or ranch horse, became medium in size, heavy-shouldered, and short-headed. He developed a pyramid-shaped neck, muscular, short flanks, and muscular forearms. The fine *criollos* seen in Argentina today are the result of a selection made from *baguales* by Dr. Emilio Solanet at his El Cardal ranch.

These *criollos* are lively and have remarkable endurance. Two such ponies, Mancha, age sixteen, and Gato, age eighteen, were ridden by the Swiss-Argentine schoolteacher Aime F. Tchiffely, from Buenos Aires to Washington, D.C. Setting out on April 23, 1925, Tchiffely and the two ponies, a piebald and a yellow dun, took two and a half years making the harrowing trip over the Andes and through the roadless jungles of Brazil and Central

America. After the 15,000-mile trek, the ponies were shipped back to pasture in Argentina. Mancha lived to the age of forty; Gato died at the age of thirty-four.

In the isolation of the Andes the Peruvian horse has developed three strains. The first is the Chola, a basic ranch horse which has a high head; straight profile; flat, broad forehead; small ears; heavy, short neck; and a rough coat either black, gray, sorrel, or dun-colored. The second type is the Costeño, a saddle horse developed from the Chola. It has style, stands about 13 or 14 hands high, and has a quiet, responsive disposition. The third type, the Morochuca, is a small, short-bodied, big-bellied, thick-necked horse adapted to the rarefied air of the high Andes.

In Venezuela the stock horse which was smaller and less stocky survived. Although it is used for ranching and is noted for its endurance, it does not gallop well and seems unable to jump into a gallop from the mark, one of the traits most needed in a good cow horse.

Brazil, which was stocked by Spanish, Dutch, and Portuguese horses, has evolved an unusual cow horse in the backland O Sertão district. This horse, of Portuguese lineage, is slight in build, has a long tail and mane, and is amazingly hardy. He has almost no vices: He seldom shies, hardly ever bucks, and he gallops very well. João do Norte, the Brazilian writer, said of this horse:

He is as plain as a Kirghiz pony. . . . He is active, though he looks lazy; agile, though he appears heavy and low-spirited; he is strong, though at first glance he seems weak. His power of resistance is extraordinary. When working with cattle he rushes through the thickest brush; jumps fallen trees, climbs high banks, stretches out or gathers himself up, springs to one side to avoid obstacles; in fact, almost works miracles.

The aridness and want of pasture stunts his growth. He seldom exceeds fourteen hands in height. He passes whole days without feed, almost without drink. His ordinary day's journey is about ten leagues, but he can manage twenty at a push. He is extraordinarily quiet. If a rider falls off he remains standing by his side.

Heavy-shouldered, short-legged, more compact horses adapted better to New World conditions and thus survived while those with "Spanish ancestor" traits died off. In Spain breeding degenerated after the sixteenth century. In America there was also little selective breeding, but that which was done was done well by unnamed trainers and veterinarians. The good reputation of the New World Spanish horse spread abroad.

The historian Francisco Cervantes Salazar, in 1544, wrote in his *Tres Diálogos Latinos,* "In spite of all, in New Spain they are raising excellent horses, horses of admirable agility and untiring nature; they are, in sum, handsomer than those of Spain."

More than 200 years later, when the thirteen colonies in North America had joined into a new union, Patrick Henry got excited about New Mexican horses and asked a friend to get him some. "Procure me two Horses and eight Mars [sic]," he wrote, "of the true Spanish blood.

Worry not about the cost of the horses nor the expense of shipping them in." A few years later, while traveling in the Americas, the Duke of Württemberg, a noted equestrian, said, "There are better horses now in Mexico than in Spain."

Perhaps the riding style and the horse needs of Mexican *vaqueros* and *charros* helped shape the *charro* horse of Mexico. The horse became something more than just an animal for transporting someone or pulling something. He turned into a high-spirited beast; an animal quick off the mark, quick to turn and to stop; an animal of marvelous calmness and exceptional intelligence. He not only worked well with men, but was a good judge of men. Mexican *charros* say of their trained horses: "Put your foot in the stirrup, and you are accurately appraised by the horse you are mounting. He is a keen judge of a man's riding ability." The horse that the *charro* helped develop was the sort of horse a Texas cowboy once bragged he owned, "A horse that can do about everything but talk and roll a Bull Durham cigarette."

As a result of natural selection and hit-and-miss breeding, such horses came into being. In size they are small, generally 14 to 15 hands high. This size seems ideal for the tasks of herding cattle, roping, and other *charro* activities. The cowman's preference for a small horse with a strong, short-coupled body is reflected in the saying of the gaucho and the *charro: Despreciar el grande, ensillar el pequeño*—"Disregard the large, saddle the small."

Perhaps the greatest difference in horse preference between the New World horsemen and their Moslem mentors is that the Arabs had a higher regard for the mare as a riding horse than for the stallion. Arabs valued the lightness and gentleness of mares. They were considered the best camp animals and were frequently kept in the family tent. Spaniards, following the European tradition, felt that the only suitable mount for a gentleman was the proud, high-spirited, powerful stallion. If the Conquistadors had had their way, perhaps only stallions would have been brought to the Americas. Thanks to the foresight of the Spanish kings and queens, a definite percentage of mares was included on each voyage to the new lands.

In breeding, the Arabs traced a horse's ancestry through the mare, a practice which the Spaniards rejected. In Mexico breeders, following the Spanish system, trace bloodline through the stallion. They believe that the mare is simply a vessel; she may give the colt some of her structure and color, but it is the stallion that imparts strong bones, vigor of nerves, solid tendons, lightness, and moral qualities. Whether one system or the other is scientifically better is questionable.

Since remote times people have believed that the color of a horse is an indicator of its physical qualities and its character. This is about as idiotic a way of judging horseflesh as it is for determining the intelligence, the goodness, or the badness of human beings by their skin or hair color. It is possible, however, as J. Frank Dobie has pointed out, that certain colors "are persistent concomitants of true breed." This simply means that certain colors, certain conformations, may indicate the horse's "race," that is, whether it is Arabian, Belgian, or Norse, just as men with certain marked physical characteristics and skin color may be African, Chinese, or Teutons.

In Latin America the selection and breeding of horses have been greatly influenced by color preferences and markings handed down by the Arabs. The Arabs prized horses that had dark or solid-color coats: chestnuts, sorrels, and dappled grays. Least desirable was the black and white pinto, probably a Barb. The Moors felt it was unlucky to ride a light bay if it had a white mane and tail. Some Moslem tribes refused to allow a light bay to remain in camp overnight.

The favorite Arabian horse was a mare without white feet or socks. If the horse had one or two white foot markings, it was considered good, especially if the left forefoot was thus marked. If the marking was on the right forefoot, it meant bad luck; most Arabs would never ride such a horse.

The importance of such markings to the Arabs, and to many *charros,* is illustrated in an anecdote about a Moorish chieftain whose prize mare was about to foal. The chief invited his friends to watch the delivery. As the colt's head first appeared, the spectators noted the well-defined white star on its head. If a horse has a white star on its forehead, Moslems consider it a good sign; if the star is irregular, it is a bad sign. Seeing the star, one of the chief's friends offered the equivalent of $100 for the colt. When the left foot of the colt appeared without any white markings on it, the value of the colt went up another $100. But as the right foot appeared with a white sock, the value of the colt dropped $100. When the rear left foot appeared with a white sock, the chieftain happily declared that he would not sell the colt at any price. Finally, when the right rear leg showed white markings, the chief became furious, swearing that the colt was valueless and he would not keep him.

A Spanish poet put these superstitions to verse:

> *Un albo, bueno;*
> *De dos, mejor;*
> *De tres es malo,*
> *Y de cuatro es peor.*

In other words:

> One white, good;
> If there are two, better;
> But three is bad,
> And four is worse.

Centuries ago both the Prophet Mohammed and Emir Abd-el-Kader fixed the color preference for the Arab world. The emir claimed that the first horse created by God was the *alazán hormiga* (dark, or ant-colored sorrel), and it had the finest qualities to be found in a horse. Mohammed himself prophesied, "Gather all Arabian horses and race them; the *alazán* will win." Another Arab added to this folklore, saying, "If someone tells you a horse jumped to the bottom of an abyss without injury, ask its color; if the reply is dark, believe it. The horse is an *alazán*—the best, the strongest, the most sober."

Many of these beliefs were carried to Mexico, playing a vital role in horse selection. In 1580 the equestrian writer Juan Suárez de Peralta wrote that the best horses in the New World were dark sorrels, dark and clear chestnuts. He added that it was a good sign if the horse had a white foot on the mounting side; if it was on the other or right side, the horse could not be as good.

Mexicans also believed that if a bay had a few white hairs in its tail, he was sure to be strong, swift, and have a good mouth. A dapple gray coat on a colt indicated that he would be fast. The cream-colored horse, on the other hand, was usually slow; a dark chestnut usually turned out swift and strong but was apt to be choleric. In Brazil's O Sertao region horsemen believed that a chestnut was good on both soft and hard ground; that a piebald was made by God to carry packs, nothing else.

The *remolinos,* or whorls of hair on a horse's hide, were almost as important as color in judging a horse in both the Arab and the New World. There are some forty whorls at different points on a horse's body. Horsemen were indifferent to twenty-eight of them, while the remainder had a prophetic influence on the animal and its owner. Six of the *remolinos* indicated good luck; among these were the whorls between the ears, on the neck, and the cinch whorls on the sides. Among the bad-luck *remolinos,* there are the ones above the eyebrows, those near the shoulder, and those beside the tail. In Mexico some of the whorls still have their Arab names, such as "the finger of the Prophet whorl" (on the neck). This extensive folklore and superstition, although colorful, is about as useful in judging a horse as phrenology, the study of the conformation of the human head, is in understanding a man.

Mexican *charros* also developed certain other signs for determining the disposition of a horse from its physical conformations. They claimed that there were four distinct types of horses:

Type 1. This horse has a steady, benevolent gaze, a uniform, narrow head, wide forehead, and well-formed ears, which are quite separate at birth and stand up from the head at an angle (never straight up). This horse trains easily. It adapts well to varied conditions and kinds of work. It makes an ideal mount.

Type 2. If the horse has protuberances beneath its eyes, puffed cheeks, and a thick throat, it is a sign that the horse is lazy and must be worked constantly. In training it, much patience is needed. When it gets angry, it loses its senses, and no amount of harsh treatment will affect it.

Type 3. This horse has large, frightened-looking eyes which seem capable of looking to the front and back without moving the eyeball. It works with energy but is apt to be nervous and easily frightened. Although it resists training, once trained it responds well.

Type 4. The horse has a massive forehead, indicating a propensity for running away. It has a bulldog nose, ears that are set back sharply, and tiny eyes that seem treasonable. Its actions are unpredictable. It is easily angered. Tight control must be maintained over it at all times.

Whether such rule-of-thumb guides are useful is difficult to say. To the average horseman they might mean nothing, but to the *charro* and to the Arab, whose long intimacy with the horse permits them to discern qualities of spirit and intelligence that no man who regards a horse as merely a tool or as an animal for sport can comprehend, they may have more meaning.

In recent years the Mexican *charro,* although still conversant with these traditional color and marking signs, has paid more and more attention to scientific breeding in the selection of his mount. He has gone abroad—to Europe, Argentina, and the United States—searching for exemplary stock.

For the *charro*'s particular style of riding, which is agile, daring and somewhat flamboyant, the ideal horse is medium in height, somewhat stocky, muscular, well boned, and light. The neck should be wide, elevated, and rounded on each side; the forehead should be wide and solid; the face short, wide, and straight; the ears slim, arched, and not too large; the eyes should be large and lively; the nostrils black, wide, and dilated. The horse's mane should be fine, brilliant, and should fall over the neck on the mounting side. The withers should be fairly high, contributing to lightness, while the back should be as straight as possible. The chest should be deep and wide; the shoulders long and curved; the forelegs should be long and strong; the hindlegs muscular and long. The tail should be abundant, long, fine, and brilliant.

The quarter horse, developed in the Southwest of the United States by breeding the Spanish cow horse and the American colonial-bred short horse, fits the *charro* qualifications perfectly. It has speed; it has enough weight to hold a roped cow; it is unusually intelligent; it has quick starting and turning ability and great self-control.

The *charro* seeks all these attributes in his horse. And, in addition, he wants his horse to be a dark sorrel; if there are any markings, there should be a well-defined star on the forehead and a white foot on the mounting side.

7 Saddle and Gear

A Mexican ranch song has the refrain "The *charro*'s saddle is the son of Spain and the nephew of Arabia." We might add, the *charro*'s saddle is the father of our Western, or stock, saddle.

If you were a young sixteenth-century Spaniard getting ready for an adventure in the new lands Columbus had just discovered and you were assembling your equipment, there would be quite an array of saddles to choose from. For the *a la brida* style of riding, still popular at the turn of the century, there were three saddles: the *silla de croata,* used for everyday riding; the *silla de estradiota,* used by the semi-armored cavalrymen; and the *silla de armas,* employed by knights. This latter war saddle had metal fenders which partially enclosed the thighs of the rider; both the knight and the horse were fully armored and together made an ambulating fortress.

If you preferred the *a la jineta* school of riding, you also had a choice of three saddles. On the *silla de gala,* an ornate version of the Arab saddle, the seat was covered with velvet, the trapping with gold and silver, and the stirrups were highly varnished. There was also a *silla para caballeros,* a gentleman's saddle, just a little less ornate. Finally there was the *silla de campo,* the Spanish cattleman's modification of the Arab saddle. It retained the high Moorish cantle, but the front of the tree was raised and narrowed, suggesting the beginnings of the American pommel.

If you were practical, looking for a good work saddle, the latter would be the saddle you would choose for adventuring in the New World. This was the saddle Cortés and his men took to Mexico. But arriving in America, you, like the other colonists, would find reasons to modify this saddle; lengthening the stirrups for more comfortable riding over great distances, then changing the saddle's shape to suit the demands of a new style of ranching.

Within thirty years after Cortés had landed at Veracruz the first distinctly American saddle took shape. At first the colonizers relied on Spanish saddlemakers, but this task was soon taken over by Indian craftsmen who better understood the needs of the ranchers. How this change began to occur was told by an eyewitness, Father Jerónimo de Mendiata, in his *Historia Eclesiástica Indiana.*

Father Mendieta says that immediately after Cortés had destroyed the Aztec capital, Tenochtitlán, and buildings of Mexico City rose phoenixlike from its ruins, the first Spanish harness and saddlemaker arrived in the city. His name was Alonzo Martínez. It was the custom at that time, since so few people could read and write, for shopkeepers to advertise their wares with some sort of symbol hung in front of the shop: A barber hung out a brass shaving bowl; a dairy shop hoisted a white flag; the butcher, a red flag; a shoemaker displayed a wooden shoe. To call attention to his trade, Alonzo Martínez displayed a wooden saddletree above his door.

One day, having done a good morning's work, Alonzo Martínez shut his shop in order to have lunch. As he closed the wooden door shutters, he noticed that the street was almost deserted; only a few Indians loitered in the distance. However, while he was at lunch, the Indians came to the shop door, where they boosted one of their number so he could take down Alonzo's saddletree.

When the saddlemaker discovered the theft, he went to the municipal officials, complaining about the robbery. To his annoyance the officials treated the matter lightly. "After all, it was just a wooden saddletree," they said. "You can make another easily."

The following day, when Alonzo opened his shop doors, he discovered that the original saddletree was again hanging in its place over the doorway. He thought the city officials, after all, had done something about the theft. But he questioned it no further.

A week later, when he had almost forgotten about the incident, an Indian appeared in his shop carrying a half-dozen saddletrees, exact copies of the one above the door. The Indian offered to sell them to Don Alonzo at a ridiculously low price. He also said that he had more of them at home, but if Don Alonzo didn't want them, he'd sell them to someone else. The saddlemaker's rage was monumental, and there was good reason for it—soon Indian artisans became the principal saddlemakers of Mexico.

Although New World saddlemakers made numerous minor changes in the saddle, the most important change was their development of the saddle horn, or pommel. It converted the saddle from being merely a seat into becoming a functional tool of the cattle industry. It changed the horse from a simple riding animal into a man's working partner. Without the pommel much of the most colorful history of Mexico and the southwestern United States would never have been written.

To understand the importance of the pommel, one must realize that until its invention, when cows were roped (usually by the horns), the herder had to dismount and control the cow with his own weight and manpower. If the cow or bull was fairly docile, the herder then tied the rope to his horse's tail, remounted, and led the animal away—if the animal agreed to go. The capped pommel changed all this. It provided a capistan around which a rope could be wound to serve as a pulley; it allowed the rider to remain mounted and to make use of the horse's strength and weight in controlling cattle.

The Mexican, or *charro,* saddle, which evolved from the Spanish-Moorish saddle, has as its base the *fuste,* or saddletree, a strongly built hardwood frame with a transverse cantle, a forebow to which the pommel is bolted, and the seat. This whole framework is covered with rawhide stretched into shape. The structure is set upon a broad, curved, sole-leather plate which rests on the horse's back. The plate, called *los bastos* (skirts), is usually lined with undressed lambskin. The saddle is fixed to the animal by a broad, short band of coarsely woven horsehair or cotton cordage—the cinch—which passes under the belly at a point approximately even with the stirrups. At each end of the cinch are metal rings through which the *latigo,* or cinch straps, tighten the cinch to horse and saddle. Hanging from the saddletree on each side are the adjustable *arciones,* or stirrup leathers, which are wide and often beautifully decorated. At their lower end are the *estribos,* or stirrups, made of metal or wood and covered with leather.

The *charro* saddle, with its sturdy pommel capable of withstanding a tremendous pulling strain, with its absence of forebow, with its flat seat, and with its low cantle which allows a roper to move away from an awkward throw, differs greatly from the gaucho saddle of the Argentine and the present-day American stock saddle. The gaucho saddle, called *el recaudo,* is basically the medieval *a la brida* adapted to the needs of the pampas. The *a la jineta* saddle never reached south of the Amazon on the Atlantic side of the continent.

As the traditional *charro* saddle was ridden northward into Texas, American horsemen again shaped it to their needs. In Texas the Mother Hubbard, or early Western, saddle followed the lines of the *charro* saddle. It was low and open, having a low cantle, a right-angle horn, and no swells in the forebow.

Farther west, the Pueblo saddle of the 1870's developed a high, dish-shaped cantle, a small, upright nickel horn, and large square skirts. Still farther west, the Californians made a compromise between the Mother

Hubbard and the Pueblo saddles, creating their own seat which was noted for its exceptionally long *tapaderos* (the leather covering the stirrups) and its unobtrusive round skirt. It became the standard saddle in California, Nevada, and Oregon, as well as parts of Arizona and Idaho.

The present-day Western saddle, although still retaining some Mexican features, is a poorly designed offspring of the earlier Western saddles. Saddlemakers abandoned the Mexican saddletree and, during the last fifty years, have continually built up the seat, turning it into a kind of bucket affair. Horseman John Richard Young calls these contemporary saddles "feed troughs with cinches." With their stirrup leathers set too far forward the rider sits behind his stirrups rather than over them. The shape of the seat also thrusts the rider back against the cantle, making it impossible for him to maintain a well-balanced seat.

Even in Mexico the traditional *charro* saddle undergoes continual changes. For roping work during *charreada* contests many Mexican horsemen have adopted a saddle with a narrower pommel, designed by Ernesto Icaza and popularized by the noted *charro* Don Juan Zaldívar. Ranchers, however, still prefer the less elegant, sturdier pommel for the hard work of the range.

In addition to various modifications of the saddle's shape, the ways of decorating the saddle have varied greatly from one period to another. The Spanish colonial horsemen, like the new-rich everywhere, delighted in displaying their wealth. There was a great deal of keeping up with the Joneses or outdoing them where saddles were concerned. Shortly after the Conquest, when Nuño de Guzmán, a representative of the king, arrived in Mexico, Cortés' lieutenant, Pedro de Alvarado, presented Guzmán with a handsome saddle; its seat was covered with white silk, the skirts were dotted with pearls, the stirrup leathers were inlaid with gold and fine enamel work, and the harness was made of morocco leather and velvet embroidered with gold and silver thread.

Such ostentation got so out of hand, with horsemen sinking fortunes in their saddles, that in 1623 King Philip IV tried to prohibit what he called "the scandalous sumptuosity of the colonists." He was hardly successful. Riders, like modern car owners, enjoy putting on the dog. The word *charro,* which today simply means a horseman, originally meant an ill-bred, showy, flashy person.

In New Mexico, by 1846, the saddle had become a kind of horse-borne treasure house. New Mexican saddles had hundreds of pounds of precious decorations on them. The high pommel was crowned with solid silver; the cantle was inlaid with silver. Wherever a bit of leather showed, it was embroidered with drawn gold or drawn silver thread. Bits were inlaid with gold, and the bridle was made of woven silver wrought in fanciful designs. The *cola de pata,* or *anquera,* a stiff leather canopy covering the entire haunch of the horse and attached to the cantle, was beautifully tooled, embroidered with silver thread, as well as adorned with pendent decorations and silver bells that tinkled as the animal moved. The purpose of this fanciful bit of gear was to protect the animal's rear from wounds and to raise or help posture its tail.

Charro ostentation was not limited to Mexican horsemen. A Californian and former forty-niner, D. W. Thompson, set a record for flamboyant saddles. His parade saddle was made of Mexican leather, hand-tooled in incomparable style. It was richly decorated with silver hammered or drawn from Mexican silver dollars. Each part of the saddle was bordered with rows of beautifully fashioned silver rosettes; the pommel was encased in solid silver; the cantle and stirrups were almost solid silver inlay. The reins, throat latch, romal, and martingale were made of silver dollars that had been cold-drawn into fine silver wire, then woven into sections joined by solid silver rings. The bridle was covered with fluted silver, except the cross band, which consisted of two slender silver chains that crossed the horse's face under a silver six-point star. The bridle alone weighed 12 pounds and had more than 250 silver dollars in it.

Nowadays a well-to-do *charro* may own two saddles: an ornate one (although not quite as gaudy as the ones described above) for parades and festive occasions; and a functional, traditional *charro* saddle upon which he does most of his chores and exhibition riding.

The *charro*'s other gear, called *montadura,* consists of bridle and bits, the *anquera* (already described), his quirt, his serape, the machete, and pistols.

Most important of the gear, of course, are the bridle and bit. Like the *charro* saddle, the bit is Arabian in origin. Its Spanish name, *freno,* meaning a brake, vividly describes its function. The most common Spanish bit, often called spade bit, from the spade-shaped piece of metal that exerted pressure against the palate of the horse when the reins were pulled, was an instrument of latent torture. Used by a skilled rider, it did not necessarily torture the animal. As the cowboy historian, Philip Ashton Rollins has pointed out, its function was to suggest physical suffering rather than to cause it. A horse knowing what such a bit could do, and being bridled, turned to the right or left at the slightest pressure of the reins on his neck. "A strand of yarn would have sufficed to guide the beast."

Charros today use a less harsh bit. This soft bit, a modification of the old Spanish bit, has a solid copper, curved pressure piece. The cheek pieces, to which the reins are attached, are elaborately fashioned and often decorated with gold or silver inlay.

8 The Well-Dressed Horseman

There are few places in the world where the specialized clothing of horsemen is as distinctive and colorful as in Mexico. Furthermore, no equestrian styles have so closely reflected the dramatic history of a country as the dress of the *charro*.

The clothes of Mexico's early *charros* resulted from Spain's effort to prevent her colonies from competing with the textile industries in the motherland. Although cotton was native to Mexico (the Indians had been weaving it into fine cloth 1,000 years before the Conquest) and though millions of sheep were producing good wool in the New World a half century after Cortés landed at Veracruz, Spain restricted the local manufacture of these products into quality fabrics. The only cloth local weavers were allowed to make was a cheap muslin and a rough homespun with which to clothe the Indians.

Since these crude textiles neither were very strong nor offered much protection against the elements, Mexican *vaqueros* and ranchers searched for some other material capable of withstanding hard usage on the range. They finally settled upon the light, tough, comfortable *gamuza,* that is, any of the suede or chamoislike skins of animals. The first garment they made of this was a simple poncho fashioned of a single skin, having a slit cut in the center for the wearer's head to go through. Eventually the sides were laced or sewn up; then sleeves were added. In time this evolved into a fitted jacket.

The same occurred with *gamuza* trousers. The first ones were a kind of primitive chaps to protect the leg. Originally they were about knee length, but by the eighteenth century they had lengthened to the ankle and were fastened up the sides with silver buttons. The wearers of these leather garments were known as *los cuerudos*—the leather-covered ones. The men who wore these outfits were herders, ordinary cowboys and small ranchers. The only luxuries they displayed in their dress were the undergarments: spotless white, long underpants and shirts of cotton. The shirts were often pleated and beautifully embroidered. To add a touch of color, *los cuerudos* sometimes wore a red sash about the waist and sported a red bandana at the neck.

In New Mexico and California horsemen had their own distinctive costumes. The Californian wore his hair long, parted in the middle, braided on each side so that his ears were exposed. His sideburns, called *orilla de la quijada,* were extremely long, yet the rest of his face was shaven (at least on Saturdays). He wore a head bandana of black silk knotted at the back and, atop his head, a broad-brimmed sombrero of palm weave, secured with silk ribbons or a deerskin band. The wealthy Californian used a felted wool or vicuña sombrero.

The New Mexican horseman's sombrero was also wide-brimmed and low-crowned. It was often covered with oil-cloth and was encircled with a band of tinseled cord an inch in diameter. His jacket was handsomely decorated with embroidery and silver braid and was held together with barrel buttons. His underdrawers were starched and white. His trousers were peculiarly cut; the outer side of the leg was open from hip to ankle and was bordered with embroidery and filigree buttons. His leggings were made of embossed leather embroidered with silk and silver threads and bound at the knee with curious tasseled gaiters.

During Spain's 300-year domination in the New World the *criollos,* native-born sons of Spanish settlers, and the *mestizos,* mixed-blood sons of Spaniards and Indians, were restricted as to the fabrics they could wear, as well as to the ornateness of their costumes.

The wealthier, pure-blooded colonists, especially the owners of large haciendas, wore elegant costumes. The short jacket was usually made of dark-blue or gray velvet. The front of the jacket was open and had long lapels of a contrasting color. The trousers, also of velvet, were slit up the sides and decorated with embroidery and silver buttons. The sombrero for this costume was the broad, flat-brimmed, low, round-crowned style introduced from Córdoba in Spain. It resembled the present-day bullfight picador's hat. The boots were usually made of suede, either full boots or wing boots, which were open at the front and back like our present-day cow boots. A later development in the wing boot included an added piece on each side, called a *vista* (something shown), which was decorated with designs in gold thread or peacock-blue silk thread (the favorite color of the *charros*).

In the 1810 War of Independence, which freed Mexico from Spain, the small ranchers and *vaqueros* played a most important part. The war also freed them from Spanish restrictions, and as a result they went to extremes in decorating their costumes. One of the Mexican leaders, Pedro de Nava, appeared on the battlefield wearing an elegant ranch costume. He wore a finely made Cordobese-style sombrero decorated with gold; blue-velvet trousers embroidered up the sides and fastened with silver buttons; a jacket of fine deerskin embellished with silver buttons and silk embroidery.

It was also at this time, as a result of the war, that the pistol became a decorative part of the *charro* costume. Today, even though sidearms are hardly needed in ranch work, a brace of pistols remains an important part of the *charro* costume.

Following the War of Independence the *charro* costume underwent various changes in style; each region of the country added decorative embellishments or changed the shape and size of the sombrero. Then, in the 1860's when the French invaded Mexico and installed Maximilian as emperor, that ill-starred monarch added his own touch to the national costume. Desiring to identify himself with Mexican tradition, as well as to win friends, Maximilian frequently wore *charro* clothes. His costume, however, had an aristocratic touch; he wore black velvet, an impractical color never before used by ranchers. The style, nevertheless, was promptly copied by numerous horsemen with aristocratic leanings.

The one part of the *charro* outfit that Maximilian did not modify was the spurs. Although an entire book could be written on spurs, we need only mention here that the spurs brought to the Americas by the Conquistadors were smaller and less extended than the medieval knight's spurs. The spur with the large six-inch spiked rowel was developed later in Mexico and California. Tastes in *charro* spurs have varied as much as in costume. The most popular types in Mexico have been the spurs with the starlike rowels and another called *rosas* on which the points are enclosed in an undulating ring of metal giving the rowel the silhouette of a rose. Frequently the spurs have small pieces of steel called *ruidos* (noises) ringing the axis of the rowel so that they make a pleasant sound. Such spurs are said to sing; they are more highly prized than mute ones. As with bridle, bit, and saddle, the Mexican *charro* has usually embellished his spurs with fanciful inlay enamel or silver and gold chasing.

After Maximilian's death, the Mexican *charro* world developed its own kind of feudal aristocracy, which is remembered today as the Old Guard. It was made up of wealthy men who lived on and worked their large haciendas and huge ranches. Their costumes, although rich, were for the most part, practical. These men were noted for their horsemanship and their devotion to tradition. Their influence, however, lasted only a few decades and was undermined, in part, by their own sons.

The sons of the Old Guard preferred to travel and to live abroad rather than work the home range. In Europe they learned new styles of riding, including the fox hunt, and they came home with elegant ideas about how a horseman should dress. Although their equestrianship was often quite expert, it was also quite divorced from Mexican ways. They felt too important to train, even to curry their own horses; and when they worked with a lasso, there was usually a servant near at hand to coil the rope for them. In matters of dress they brought home refinements unheard of before: the English "break" at the trouser cuff, longer jackets, narrower lapels, butterfly-shaped neckties, formfitting fabrics, such as cashmeres and poplins.

During the Revolution of 1910, when the entire structure of Mexican society was torn apart, the Old Guard and their elegant sons disappeared. At the same time, it seemed as if the *charro* traditions of Mexico would vanish, too. For years chaos prevailed: Good horse breeders abandoned their ranches; skilled saddlemakers, bootmakers, hatmakers, and *charro* tailors died. Furthermore, no one seemed interested in maintaining the uniquely Mexican school of riding.

Although the costume of the *charro* did not altogether disappear during the post-revolution period, it fell into the hands of theatrical people who cheapened it. The *charro's* outfit came to signify something even gaudier than the original Spanish meaning of the word. It became the costume of mariachi musicians in nightclubs and of

Mexican movie cowboys and of waiters in Mexican restaurants. They popularized the gaudy jackets decorated with garish Aztec calendars and Indian heads; the neckties that resembled tiny blankets; the bright artificial-silk shirts covered with tasteless embroidery; the out-size sombreros which no good horseman or roper in his right mind would use.

Fortunately, as often happens when a rich tradition is threatened with extinction, some men will devote all their energies to keep it alive or revive it. This happened in Mexico. The handful of men interested in Mexican riding and its traditions, who banded together in *charro* clubs a few decades ago, not only have helped improve Mexican horse breeds, but have focused interest on their country's traditional riding and the costumes that go with it.

The Mexican girls, who play a brilliant equestrian role in a Mexican *charreada,* have their own traditional costumes. Although their dress has gone through fewer changes than the male costume, its origin is related to an interesting legend.

The most popular version of this legend is that during the late seventeenth century some English pirates captured a Chinese ship in the Pacific, and part of the booty taken was a lovely Mongol princess named Mina. She was sold into slavery and eventually became the property of Don Miguel Sosa, a Mexican living in Puebla. Don Miguel, being kindly and pious, had the girl baptized and educated. Although he showered her with jewels and finery, none of this impressed the girl. She had become such a good Christian that she gave everything to the poor and was content to wear a simple skirt of red flannel, a plain white blouse, and a native *rebozo,* or shawl. This outfit, called the *china poblana,* has become the riding and fiesta costume of the *charros'* women. The word *china,* now seldom used, once meant servant girl; *poblana* is the nickname of people living in Puebla.

Following *charro* traditions, the costume is now somewhat more elaborate than that worn by the Mongol princess. The red, long skirt is adorned with a quantity of sequins, while the upper ten inches of the skirt is colored green, so that with the white blouse the combination completes the colors of the Mexican flag. The outfit is finished off with red or green shoes, a red or green *rebozo,* and a typical *charro* sombrero.

Both girl and men riders usually have a folded or rolled serape, or narrow blanket, tied behind the cantle of the saddle. The fringe always hangs down the mounting side of the horse.

When combined, the spirited horse, the *charro,* and the *china poblano* in their vivid dress, the handsome saddle, and the distinctive gear all contribute to a magnificent spectacle—the *charreada.* It has the excitement of a Wild West rodeo, the color of an opera, the grace of a ballet.

9 The Charreada

When we speak of a national sport, we usually mean a sport or athletic contest that is typical of a particular country. It need not be the most popular sport indulged in by people of that country. Europeans think of baseball as being distinctly North American. We look upon golf as the national sport of the Scots, cricket as being a typically English game. Although soccer attracts more spectators in Mexico, riding and the *charreada* might be called the typical national sport.

More than any other sports competition the *charreada* reflects the spirit and traditions of Mexico: her history, her taste in dress, her love of horses, and her flair for the dramatic. Says José Alvarez del Villar:

> There is a bit of the *charro* in every Mexican. There is a sensitive filament in our beings which responds to Mexican music . . . to the sight of a horse well-ridden, to the spectacle of a bull skillfully lassoed. . . . All of us, absolutely all of us, share the national feeling for horsemanship.

90

The rodeolike *charreada* was not the product of any one person's imagination; it simply grew with Mexico. Some of its roots go back to the Spanish colonial period, to the *alardes,* or militia types of reunions instituted right after the Conquest. Although these assemblies were for the purpose of impressing the Indians with Spain's military power, the horsemen who gathered together used the opportunity to enjoy themselves and to display their riding skills.

In addition to the *alardes,* certain other equestrian games, imported from Spain and popular during the colonial period, contributed to the development of the *charreada* contests. Certainly the most colorful and exciting game was called *canas* (meaning, cane or javelin). It was derived from the Arabian light-cavalry exercise called *el jerida.* In it two teams of from four to ten riders would stage a mock battle, throwing light bamboo canes or javelins at one another. The riders exhibited every trick of horsemanship they knew to evade the javelins thrown by the opposition or to catch the javelins in midair and hurl them back. Colonial documents of the period show that a great deal of money and effort was expended in turning these games into brilliant fiestas; elaborate grandstands were constructed and decorated with silks and banners imported from the Orient.

In smaller cities and provincial towns still another game, derived from the medieval tournaments of the knights, was equally popular. This game was called *sortijas,* or tournament of rings. Instead of knights battling each other with lances and battle-axes, the colonial riders used light lances to snare rings made of colored ribbons that were hung overhead along a racecourse. To add a romantic touch to the game, each ribbon ring was a certain color and represented a particular girl in the town. Competition for the rings representing the most beautiful girls was intense, because the girl was expected to shower favors upon the winner.

In the tournament of rings a rider could be disqualified or penalized for various faults — a foreshadowing of the strict rules governing today's *charreadas*. For a *sortija* a horseman was required to use a small horse and the *a la jineta* saddle. He could hold the reins only in the left hand. If he lost his stirrup, his hat, or his cape, he received further penalties.

Although such competitive games contributed to the *charreada,* the most important influence on its form and style was the work of the ranch, especially the routines of branding and roundups. During the annual roundups on Mexican ranches, countless years before there was a ranch in Texas or California, men rode in from long distances to help with the branding. After the work was completed, the horsemen celebrated. There was food, dancing, music, and, above all, competitions in which riders displayed their skills at roping, riding wild horses, and throwing bulls by the tail.

These celebrations became an important part of the living tempo on large haciendas. They were, in a sense, a safety valve relieving the tensions and the monotony of an existence that offered little in the way of entertainment. The *charreadas* held on haciendas even fascinated men hardly cut out to be cowboys. Who can picture an Episcopalian or Roman Catholic bishop jumping down from the grandstand at an American rodeo to ride a bucking bronco? This happened in Mexico.

A scandalous example of such indulgence in earthly pleasures was set by His Eminence Don Pelasio de Labastida, an eighteenth-century bishop of Mexico City. This vigorous man often slipped away from his episcopal duties and went to nearby Cuernavaca, where, flinging aside his clerical robes and dignity, he tailed wild bulls and lassoed mares. Nor was he the only clergyman to take part in *charreadas.* In 1700 the Archbishop of Michoacán had to issue a stern proclamation forbidding the clergy to throw bulls and to ride bucking horses at ranch fiestas—too many of them were risking their necks.

During the eighteenth and nineteenth centuries the horsemen's competitions, especially on haciendas and ranches, became more and more fixed in form. The techniques of specialized exhibitions were refined—the method of tossing a bull, the styles of roping, the rules for riding wild horses and cattle. By the beginning of the twentieth century almost all the events you see in a modern-day *charreada* had been developed. On the haciendas the *charreada* fiestas reached a kind of crescendo under the guidance of the Old Guard *charros.* At times hundreds of horsemen would gather and take part in such a fiesta.

Following the Revolution (1910—1917), when Mexico finally quieted down, people renewed their interest in the *charreada*—but with a startling difference. Instead of the sons of hacienda owners and ranchers reviving the old riding traditions, the upper-middle-class city dwellers took over. Engineers, lawyers, doctors, and other professional men, as well as some modern ranchers, banded together in town after town to preserve the old *charro* traditions. The *charreada* moved from the range country into the city.

Once in the hands of urban riders, *charro* riding ceased to be an easygoing pastime; it became an exacting, rugged sport that demanded constant training and practice on the part of its participants. The competitions became so stiff that detailed rules of procedure had to be set up. At the same time, having moved into the city, the *charreada* demanded a proper setting in which to stage the competitions. The irregular ranch corral would no longer do.

In the 1920's the *charro* club in Mexico City constructed the first frying-pan-shaped amphitheater, or *lienzo,* and it set the pattern for the numerous *charreada* plazas that have since been built throughout the country. Each has its ring (properly called the *plaza*) with a small grandstand at one end and a judge's stand on the opposite side of the ring; and each has its alleyway (called *lienzo*), with the necessary corrals for cattle and wild horses, as mentioned. Although the basic shape of the amphitheater is always the same, the dimensions may vary considerably. Some, including ring and alleyway, are almost 100 yards long. Experts are agreed, however, that the ideal overall length should be about 75 to 80 yards long. The ring itself should not measure more than

12 yards in diameter. If there is but a single alleyway, it may measure 15 or 20 yards across. In more elaborate amphitheaters there may be two runways, or *lienzos:* one for ropers to work in, the other for tailing bulls.

During a formal *charreada* in a first-class amphitheater there may be several groups of judges equipped with stopwatches and scoring pads. Some are specialists in judging the roping events, others the riding events. In small Mexican towns the weekly competitions are less formal; judges may not be present, and frequently some of the events are eliminated.

If you attend a full-scale *charreada* in Mexico, especially in Guadalajara, in Mexico City, or at the famous San Marcos fair at Aguascalientes, here is a brief listing of what you will see. A more detailed description of the events is included in later chapters.

Usually before riding to the amphitheater for the day's competition, the competing *charros* attend a religious service in a chapel connected with their club headquarters or at a nearby church. Arriving at the amphitheater, the horsemen and horsewomen enter the ring through a special gate and parade before the grandstand in all their finery. A speech of welcoming is offered to the guest of honor and the spectators; then the riders take positions around the rim of the ring.

1. *Cala de caballos*: This is usually the first event, in which riders exhibit their control over and the training of their horses.

2. *Concurso de peales:* Roping running mares by their

hind feet, from horseback and on foot. This event is usually staged in the wide alleyway.

3. *Colas or coleares*: A bull or steer is released in the runway, and a *charro* must grab his tail and throw the beast upon its back within a given number of yards and given time. It is one of the most exciting of the events.

4. *Jineteo de novillo*: Bareback riding on a wild bull or steer.

5. *Jineteo de yeguas*: Riding a wild mare bareback and with saddle. Every *charro* is expected to try his hand at this and the bull-riding event.

6. *Jarabe tapatio*: Usually to change the pace of the events and to add a touch of color, a wooden platform is set up in the ring upon which a couple—*charro* and *china poblana*—or a group of dancers do the *jarabe,* the Mexican hat dance, as well as other folk dances.

7. *Manganas a pie*: A roping event in which the *charros,* on foot, lasso the front feet of a running mare.

8. *Manganas a caballo*: The *charros* on horseback compete in roping the front feet of a running mare.

9. *Paso de la muerte*: This event, called the ride of death, is aptly named. Several riders drive a wild mare ahead of them around the ring. The performing *charro* races parallel to the mare, leaping from his horse to her back, riding her bareback.

10. *Escaramuza*: A exhibition of precision maneuvers and formation riding done by groups of girls riding sidesaddle. If such an exhibition is included in the *charreada* you attend, then you have hit a jackpot, because there

are less than a half-dozen groups of girl riders trained in this dangerous, exacting art.

11. *Rejonear*: This is also a bonus event reserved for very special *charreadas*. The word *rejonear* means to fight a bull from horseback. Only a perfectly trained horse and horseman can perform this event, because the beast they oppose is a carefully bred, heavy, fast, fighting bull. The horseman works without touching the reins, maneuvering his horse through graceful, precise, and beautiful figures as he evades and closes in on the bull.

10 The Riding Events

In a *charreada* the first competitive event is the *cala de caballo*. The competing horseman rides across the ring, salutes the guests in the grandstand; then he backs his mount from the ring into the alleyway, covering the entire distance he intends for his exhibit, perhaps 60 to 90 yards.

Now, receiving a signal from the judges, he urges his horse into a breakneck gallop toward the grandstand, where, just as it appears that he will crash into it, he brings his horse to a halt in three stages called *rayar* (to mark or gouge). In each of these three braking actions the horse seems to crouch on his haunches, sliding forward, then crouching, then sliding forward. At last the horse must stand erect, absolutely quiet, facing the grandstand.

On a signal from his rider, the horse begins a series of dancing maneuvers. First, with his back legs firmly fixed to an axis spot, the animal dances to the left, then to the right, or makes a complete circle. These various figures

are called *cabriolas* (capers). The half circle to left or
right is a *media cabriola*; the full turn with the hind legs
fixed to one spot is a *cabriola natural*; a full circle with
the rear of the horse circling around the planted front
legs is a *cabriola inversa*.

Having completed these handsome capers, the rider
dismounts and remounts, the horse remaining absolutely
still as he does this. Finally the horseman makes his
mount pace backward to the starting line. Neither the
man nor animal must glance backward, and the pacing
is done as smoothly and swiftly as if the horse were going forward.

In this exhibition the horseman's score can be cut
down owing to various faults. The rider loses points if the
horse hesitates before obeying a command, if he opens
his mouth, if he fails to back up smoothly and in a
straight line. At no time should the *charro* touch the
saddle pommel, lose his sombrero, or lose either stirrup.
Following the initial gallop, the horse must come to a
dead stop; the slightest movement in considered a fault.

For a horse to respond so perfectly calls for endless,
patient training. The rider cannot rely on a heavy-handed
use of reins and bit or on spurs. Proper bitting on the
neck is important, as are proper leg and boot signals. In
training his mount to the *cabriolas,* the horseman ac-
customs his beast to pressures of his leg or hand. To
make the horse *cejar,* that is, pace backward smoothly,
the rider pulls back on the reins gently and at the same
time exerts leg pressure alternately on each side, just behind the cinch. As he presses with his left leg, the horse's

left leg goes backward; pressure with the right leg makes the animal's right leg move backward. The rider, in a sense, is walking backward with his horse.

Although the ideal of every Mexican *charro* is to own a spirited, intelligent, responsive, and perfectly trained mount, this does not mean that the man is incapable of riding animals far less docile. The *charreada* features bucking-horse and wild-steer riding. These events are lumped under the name *jineteos*. As is done in American rodeos, the animals may be ridden bareback or saddled; however, in Mexico, instead of the rider dropping on the beast's back as it leaves a chute or pen as is customary in the United States, the *charro* mounts the animal in the open ring.

Since most of the Mexican riders are not professional broncobusters or showmen but are simply amateurs or sportsmen, there is no attempt to use animals that are especially vicious or made dangerous. The wild mares that are ridden are taken directly from the range. They may be wicked, or they may be fairly easy to handle. They are roped and saddled in the ring. No flank straps are pulled tight, far back of the horse's belly, to torture and bring out the wickedness in him; the flank straps used in American rodeos can turn a docile horse, even a family buggy horse, into a wild kicker. You will know the strap is being used if you notice that the horse keeps his head up and tries to kick the rider off. This is not true bucking; the animal is merely using his hindquarters and is trying to kick loose the flank strap.

Occasionally a horse may be a natural bucker. The

most famous of such animals was the Chugwater, Wyoming, horse named Steamboat. He was so gentle a child could play between his legs, but let a saddle be tossed on his back and he became a barrel of firecrackers. He bucked up so straight and came down so hard that he jolted a rider apart. During his lifetime only two men ever managed to stay on him for more than a few seconds.

When riding a bull or steer, the *charro* may elect to do this freehanded or to use a *pretal* (bellyband or rope) or a neck rope to hold on with. The animal is lassoed and held down in the ring until the band is placed in position. The rider is not allowed to mount the animal while it is being held down but must leap aboard as it is freed and gets up. There are several ways of holding on to the *pretal*: The band may have a loose piece which the rider can grip with one or both hands, or he can grasp the tight band with hands reversed. This is the most dangerous method, because the man, unable to disengage his hands, may be thrown. When riding a bull or wild steer, the horseman usually ties the rowels of his spurs so they will not move; thus he can get a better grip with them on the flanks of the beast.

Sometimes for kicks two *charros* will leap upon the same steer, sitting face-to-face.

The most exciting of the wild-horse riding events is *paso de la muerte*, in which a *charro* leaps from his own running horse to the back of a wild mare. This event dramatizes a way of life once led by a remarkable breed of Mexican riders known as *mesteñeros*, or mustangers. Undoubtedly the best picture of a *mesteñero* at work is the description given by an old-time New Mexican cattle-man, Jack Thorp.

One day while riding on the open range, Thorp and some friends spied a large band of mustangs approaching them at an angle. They saw two riders crowding the band of wild horses. One of the riders was a young girl mounted on a white horse. Her saddle was a sheepskin pad.

As Thorp watched, the girl raced at incredible speed beside a sorrel mustang. "They were going like the wind," observed Thorp. Presently, when the girl got into the position she wanted, she reached over, grabbed the sorrel's mane and slipped neatly from her own horse to the back of the wild mustang. All that she carried with her was a ten-foot hair rope. As the sorrel galloped ahead, the girl threw a small loop over the animal's head, tightened it, then threw two half hitches around his nose. With only this noseband to guide the horse, she made the mustang veer out of the racing herd. "Then," said Thorp, "she vanished from sight."

Immediately after the girl had changed horses, the boy riding with her caught the reins of her white horse. He joined Thorp's group.

"How is that girl going to stop her horse?" Thorp asked the Mexican boy. "He's liable to run her into the Gulf of Mexico, no?"

"She'll come back. She is my sister," said the boy.

To Thorp's amazement the girl not only returned, but came back on the wild mustang which had never felt a human hand or a rope until that wisp of a girl—she was only fourteen years old—had skimmed to its back. Doing the *paso de la muerte* was a daily task for both the girl and her brother who were members of a Mexican family of mustangers. They made their living catching wild horses and selling them in Chihuahua.

For Mexican riders an equally exciting event in the *charreada* is the *cola,* or bull-tailing stunt. The technique of catching a steer by the tail and deftly throwing it upon its back is a distinctly Mexican show. No one knows who the first bull tosser was; perhaps some frustrated *vaquero* who was unable to stop an animal in any other way. In the colonial chronicle of Father Alonzo Ponce we find a vivid description of what may have been one of the earliest *colas.*

Father Ponce wrote:

On the Saturday of December 6, 1586, while traveling across a large plain [in Jalisco, Mexico], I saw a rider on a mare racing after a bull. Catching up with the beast, he struck it such a blow with a club that he brought it to earth. The rider set out after another bull which was faster and larger than the first one. He gave this one several blows; it staggered, fell, then rose and ran off again. Exasperated, the rider finally caught it by the tail and turned the animal with such force it lost its balance and went down.

By the end of the sixteenth century this method of downing cattle was widespread in Mexico. It was used until the techniques of cattle roping replaced it. Although no longer practiced on the range, bull tailing has remained an important event in ranch fiestas and *charre-adas*. Its appeal, even to highly cultured men, is curious. Before California became an American territory, the handsome, well-educated governor of the province, Don Mariano Guadalupe Vallejo, was a passionate bull tailer. On one occasion he and his brothers, Juan Antonio and Salvador, arranged a total of twelve bulls in three files of four animals per file. The bulls were spaced about 150 yards apart and held until a contestant approached them. Each of the brothers raced down a file, vying with one another to see who could toss four bulls the fastest. It was a remarkable feat, considering the distance, the speed of the bulls, and the absence of a walled-in runway to keep the animals from veering off.

In the early days this feat was executed by raising the bull's tail to the level of the pommel, or even using the pommel for leverage, and pulling. A little later *charros* began twisting the animal's tail around their legs, at the knee, for leverage. Nowadays the feat is performed by raising the leg and stirrup and hooking the animal's tail around the leg between the rider's calf and ankle. This is called *colear arcion de bolero*.

When you attend a *charreada,* there are a number of fine points you should be on the lookout for, because there is much more to tailing a bull than merely tossing it on its back.

Before the event begins, you may notice that the competing riders walk and gallop their horses the length of the alleyway, or *lienzo*. This is done to familiarize the horse with the ground. When the event is about to begin, the rider positions his horse parallel to the short wall at the corral end of the alleyway, head facing the gateway where the bull will come out. The wall is high enough so the horse cannot see or sense the bull in the corral and become nervous.

At the precise moment that the bull is hazed out of the corral and into the *lienzo* by other riders, the competing rider is off the mark, racing beside the bull, keeping the animal between the rider and the alleyway wall. The rider must not lag behind, because there is always the danger that the bull might swerve across his path, tumbling horse, rider, and bull.

While racing in this manner, the rider lifts his right hand, touching the back of it to his sombrero. This salute notifies the judges and timekeeper that the rider is about to tail his bull and that he is not touching his saddle horn or the horse's mane. The contestant now brings his hand down, slapping the bull on the back three times. This is done to see if the bull will veer from his course, kick, or defend himself in some other way. If the animal pursues a straight course, the rider reaches forward, places his palm on the bull's back, then slides his hand along the spine to the animal's tail. Grabbing the tail, he lets it slip through his fingers until he holds the end of it. The rider now swings his legs and stirrup up, hooking it around the tail. He veers his horse away from the bull and pulls, upsetting the bull.

Each of these actions is done at a thundering gallop. The timing is split-second. The entire action, including the throwing of the bull, occurs in three to five seconds; the ground covered is between 40 to 60 yards.

The competing *charros* are judged not only on the time and distance it takes them to upset a bull but also on their style in doing it. Points are deducted from their scores for various faults. Some of the more important faults are to start from the mark before the bull has fully entered the *lienzo*; to touch the saddle or horse's mane with either hand; to use the quirt on the horse; to raise the leg more than once in hooking the tail; to raise the leg too high (it must be done at the level of the stirrup leathers); to look toward the sky or away from the bull when tailing; to lose a stirrup; or to lose a sombrero.

This is the accepted way of tailing a bull. Sometimes, however, to add spice to a *charreada,* horsemen will perform unusual variations of the *colas.* A difficult variation is to release two bulls in the alleyway side by side, with two riders pursuing them, each grabbing a tail and simultaneously veering off in opposite directions to toss their bulls. This event is called *colear mancuernas.* An even more dangerous variation is the *cambio de manos* (change of hands), in which a rider catches the tail with one hand, then switches it to the other hand, swerving behind and to the other side of the animal before throwing it.

One is less often likely to see the *colear a lola,* in which the horseman rides with a leg hooked over the horn, sidesaddle, then tosses the bull in the usual manner. Like the *lola,* the *querétana,* invented by two horsemen from the city of Querétaro, Miguel Domínquez and

Francisco Muñoz, is a flamboyant trick. For it two riders mount the same horse and set out after the bull. They perform the formal salute, slap the bull on the back, then the first man catches the animal's tail and hands it to his companion, who upsets the beast.

When a *charro* indulges in this exciting and dangerous form of horsemanship, he must be properly dressed for it. The fancy *charro* costumes, the silver buttons, the overlarge spurs, the decorated saddle, and embellished bridle are all put aside. He wears a jacket and trousers of *gamuza*, unadorned with buttons which might tangle with the bull's tail. His sombrero is fairly heavy, at least 14 ounces, and it is held in place by a sturdy leather chin strap. His spurs are short, small-roweled, and spiked.

More important than proper costume is the horse. Not all *charro* horses have the temperament for tailing bulls. The best horse for this event is the quarter horse, one that is unafraid of cattle, quick on the getaway, and standing about 14 to 14½ hands high. He must enjoy working with bulls, or he will be useless.

During a recent competition held at San Luis de la Paz in central Mexico, a bay, ridden by a *charro* from Mexico City, created a sensation—he was mad about bulls! Instead of holding his horse back, the rider let his mount peek around the corner of the wall separating the *lienzo* from the corral. Rather than becoming nervous at the sight or scent of the bulls, this horse seemed to get a bang out of seeing the animals he was about to pursue. Like a bird dog, whose greatest joy is to go into the field with a hunter, this horse anticipated and relished tailing bulls.

To train a horse as a perfect partner for tailing bulls, a special routine is followed. Besides the regular education given a *charro* horse, this animal receives a step-by-step course in tailing. One of the first steps is to have another rider hold the tail, taken from a bull, near the rump of his horse while the trainer and student horse follow. The tail is caught and dropped repeatedly until the horse is accustomed to the action. It is done both at a walk and finally at a gallop. Then the horse is worked with steers. He sees them rush from a corral; he learns to follow them; he watches other *charros* tail bulls. To teach the horse to make the final spurt as his rider is about to upset the bull, a second rider gives the student horse a flick on the rump with his quirt or the tip of a *reata*.

11 How to Lasso a Flying Goose

The lasso, rope, or *reata* is one of the oldest tools of the herdsman. In Europe, Asia, and the Americas, wherever men have raised cattle, they have used the rope and loop. Tartar horsemen in Asia snared the horns of cattle with nooses attached to the end of long poles; Spanish herdsmen used a similar technique. However, after an animal was roped, the herdsman usually dismounted and tied the rope to his horse's tail, then mounted and led the animal off. This was fine if you worked with domesticated cattle, but dangerous if you worked with semiwild cattle on the open range.

The Spanish colonists in the Americas hardly improved on this Old World rope technique. One of the reasons why no one hit on the trick of throwing a looped rope from horseback was that the primitive Mongolian rope and the European lasso was usually fashioned of plaited leather or woven horsehair. It lacked flexibility and body. The rope of the Mexican Indian changed this. Long before the Conquest, Mexican Indians had been manufacturing high-quality rope out of cotton and istle (the maguey, or century plant) fibers. The istle rope was unusually strong, flexible, yet it maintained a useful stiffness. This rope, capable of being thrown long distances, and the pommeled saddle gave men exceptional control over range-bred cattle and horses.

By the end of the colonial period in Latin America horsemen had developed a wonderful facility at throwing the rope and its sliding loop. They invented the *hondo,* a cunningly devised knotted or spliced eyelet lined with smooth leather or a brass ring, which let the noose slide easily along the rope. They learned to throw at great distances, snaring the front and rear legs of cattle rather than the horns. They learned to *chorrear,* or dally the rope, that is to say, loop or belay the home end of the lasso around the pommel of their saddles, smoothly paying out or tightening the rope in order to stop a captured horse or cow. Without the pommel no man could hold a rope or let it slide through his hands once he had roped cattle. A sliding rope generates terrific heat. In Tabasco a *charro* named Pedrero, after dallying out his *reata,* used to light his cigars from the smoking pommel.

In each region of the Americas men used their ropes in different ways. The Mexicans usually held the home end (opposite the loop) of their ropes free in their hand, looping it around the saddle horn a turn or two. Texans generally fastened the home end to the saddletree with a half hitch, while the Argentine gaucho tied the rope to the saddle cinch. In addition to the lasso and its loop, the gaucho adopted another curious device called the *bola.* It consists of a length of rope or rawhide with a brass ball or leather-covered stone attached to each end. It can be flung with great accuracy. When it strikes the legs of an animal, the balls whirl around, winding the cord about the legs. The *bola* was used by the Peruvian Incas long before the Spanish Conquest.

For hundreds of years almost all Mexican ranchers and *vaqueros* have been roping experts. Children grew up with ropes in their hands. They were constantly lassoing their mother's chickens, calves, ponies, and finally heavy cattle. Mexican men have used the rope not only as a tool but as a weapon. In California *vaqueros* hunted wild grizzly bears with their *reatas*: one man lassoing the animal's head, another its hind leg to immobilize the beast. In northwestern Mexico, near Chihuahua, *vaquero* ropers were such sure shots that they captured flying Canadian geese with their singing nooses.

Mexican ropers have even used their *reatas* in defense of their country. During the French invasion of Mexico, in one battle a group of Mexican *charros* swooped down on a French cannon position, firing pistols and slashing with machetes. A second group of riders whirled their ropes, lassoed the cannon, dallied their ropes around pommels, and turned the cannon over. . . . Years later, during the Revolution the lasso was again used to capture an enemy machine gun.

In the city of Querétaro people still talk about a hunt held on a huge hacienda called El Llano del Tigre. The hacienda owner, one of the Old Guard *charros,* was annoyed by some of the ideas his son had brought back from Europe. "All this chatter about hunting foxes on horseback may be well and good," he said, "but I don't like to imitate foreigners. Now let us have our own ride hunt. Since there are no foxes here, we'll hunt deer. We won't bother with dogs, nor will we use guns."

The guests he invited for the hunt were almost all ranchers. They set out in groups of three on horseback. All had agreed not to use firearms and to take only mature bucks. Before the day was over, they had captured four deer, taking them with their whirling lassos.

The Mexican *charro* selects his rope with great care. The length, thickness, and weight of the *reata* that he chooses depends on how he plans to use it. For fancy rope work, exhibition twirling, and general practice, he prefers a lightweight istle rope. If he takes part in the *mangana* events at a *charreada,* that is, lassoing the front feet of a horse, he uses his heaviest rope; for lassoing the hind feet of a horse he chooses a medium-weight rope.

No skillful roper lets anyone else loop his *reata* or condition a new rope. To prepare a newly purchased rope for use, the *charro* both suns it and stretches it. This is done by tying one end of the rope to a post or tree, then pulling and jerking it until it loses its tendency to coil. To give it further flexibility, the *charro* ties it between two trees and swings back and forth on it with all his weight. Finally, to prevent the noose, or *hondo,* from sliding too easily, about half the rope, from the noose to the middle, is rubbed with a mixture of shoemaker's wax and tar.

To snare a moving target with a lariat may appear

easy, but even the simplest throw, the one used by *vaqueros,* requires constant practice. To make this throw, you hold the portions of the coiled lariat not included in the loop in your left hand. With your right hand gripping the *hondo* and with a series of short flicks of the wrist, you pay out sufficient rope through the *hondo* to make the loop, which should be 6 or 7 feet in diameter. Now grasping the rope (loop part) about 20 inches behind the *hondo,* as well as that part of the rope which has not passed through the *hondo* to become part of the loop, you begin to revolve the loop section overhead. By the time it has made its third or fourth revolution the loop begins to take shape.

When the loop is sufficiently opened and until the throw is made, you must keep the loop steadily revolving. An instant before the throw you should give the loop several high-speed whirls. At the same time you twist your right shoulder backward and your loop-whirling hand still farther back. Then you shoot your right hand forward, releasing the loop so that it sails to meet the target. At the same time you pay out rope from the coil in your left hand as needed. With practice you can learn to shoot your loop out like a bullet or let it sail out easily and lightly.

Although every *charro* can make this traditional, direct throw, nowadays the throw is often preceded by elegant flourishes and figures made with the rope. The art of fancy rope twirling is said to have been originated toward the end of the eighteenth century by a Jalisco rancher, Don Juan Chávez. The flourishes, the caprices, the involved figures that a *charro* does with his loop as it whirls above his head, around his legs, or vertically at his side, the loop enlarging or diminishing as if by magic or spinning swiftly or fluttering as lazily as a butterfly, are very much like the musical improvisations of a composer.

In the roping events at a *charreada* the style of a *charro's* flourishes is as important as the distance and accuracy of his throw. Each roping event has its particular throws, and each throw may be accompanied by a particular flourish. The flourishes and throws each have rather colorful names.

The simplest and oldest throw, performed without any fancy flourish of the rope, is called *la vieja,* or the old one. The mask, or *la mascara,* is used to lasso a horse running from the right to the left at considerable speed. At the instant of the throw the roper twists his wrist so that the palm of his hand is facing inward as the loop is launched. *La crinolina,* which derives its name from the hoop skirt worn by eighteenth-century ladies, includes a flourish in which the loop is whirled from left to right around the roper's body, then rises upward and is launched at the target. The same flourish, but with the rope spinning in the opposite direction, is called *la contra crinolina.*

In a *charreada* competition the roper may work on horseback or on foot. He is permitted a certain number of throws, but each one must be a different style. Each kind of throw is awarded a particular number of points which the roper may lose for various reasons. He can be penalized for throwing too hastily; for losing his hat while roping; for causing a running horse to fall when it is lassoed; for failing to dally his rope properly on the pommel; and for many other infractions.

Not to be outdone by riders who perform the exciting leap from one horse to another in their *paso de la muerte,* Mexican ropers perform an equally dangerous roping trick called the throw of death. To execute this exciting throw the roper works on foot. He firmly ties his two legs together with several loops of the home end of his lariat and secures it with a slip knot. With the remainder of the rope loosely coiled in his left hand and whirling the throwing loop with his right hand, he throws a *mangana,* lassoing the hind legs of a running wild mare. As the rope is payed out, the man's legs are jerked out from beneath him, and he is dragged by the horse. When the horse finally halts, the man pulls the slipknot and stands up.

The trick is quite dangerous, requiring iron nerves, calmness, and precise timing. The man must be prepared to fall properly on his back the instant the rope jerks his legs. While being dragged, he must maintain his balance on his back, his head bent forward, watching the horse.

12 The Charro and the Cowboy

Much the same as Mexico or Argentina, the United States once had a great horse culture. Its last redoubt was in the Southwest, the great prairies, plains, and deserts stretching from the Missouri River to California. We Americans sometimes imagine that the culture of that Southwest—the cattlemen's traditions, the cowboy customs, their lingo, their clothes, their way of riding— was purely American in origin. We should realize, instead, that it was a borrowed culture.

The American rancher and cowboy learned their trades from the Mexican rancher and *charro*. They obtained all the tools of their trade from Mexicans. The saddle, bridle, lariat, spurs, chaps, and specialized apparel were merely copies of gear in use south of the Río Grande for hundreds of years before the first Americans filtered into Texas around 1821 to begin ranching. The bronco ridden by the American cowboy, the cattle that he drove, came to him by way of Mexico. Even the words that he used to designate his tools and describe his work were borrowed and since have become part of our general vocabulary.

Our word "lasso" comes from the Spanish *lazar,* meaning to rope; lariat is simply the American way of pronouncing the Spanish word for rope, *la reata.* The Texas cowpoke turned *la jaquima* into hackamore, *pinto* into paint, *mesteño* into mustang, *el cincha* into cinch, *chapareras* into chaps, and *el bronco* into bronc. Occasionally he ran into a tongue twister, so he stretched the sound a bit to make an English equivalent. He turned the Spanish word for hostler, *caverango,* into wrangler. When the Mexican *charro* showed him how to give his rope a turn around the saddle horn and said, *"Dar la vuelta*—Give it a turn," he converted the sound into a shorter word—dally.

In addition to language, tools, and clothing, we borrowed one of our liveliest, Western-style forms of entertainment, the rodeo, from the Mexican ranch fiesta and *charreada.* Since the early nineteenth century American cowboys showed off their riding, their broncobusting, and roping at fiestas of their own, usually held after roundup and branding time. It was not until much later, however, that rodeos became exhibitions of Western equestrianship for the public to enjoy.

The first organized rodeo, called a ranch show, was staged by the Miller 101 Ranch people. Although the Miller Ranch was in Oklahoma, the show was put on in Winfield, Kansas, on July 4, 1881. Soon similar riding shows were being staged everywhere: Buffalo Bill Cody organized one for his hometown, North Platte, Nebraska, in 1882; Pecos, Texas, held one the following year; and Cheyenne, Wyoming, staged the first of its still famous "Frontier Days" in 1896.

None of these ranch shows was called a rodeo until 1907–8 when the Miller 101 Ranch people brought the "Wild West" out of the West with a vengeance. Their rodeo, touring both the United States and Europe, included everything—bulldogging, fancy roping, trick riding, and bucking-bronco riding. While the show was going strong, an unknown rider and his horse were with the outfit; their names, Tom Mix and Tony.

The only event these shows failed to borrow from the Mexican *charreada* was the *charro*'s trick of tailing a bull. In its place Bill Pickett, a Negro member of the 101 Ranch and one of the greatest cowboys and rodeo performers to come out of the West, devised something just as daring—bulldogging. Pickett raced his quarter horse beside a steer, leaped from his saddle to the horns of the steer, and using the horns as levers, twisted the animal's head to throw the beast to the ground. Sometimes to hold the animal better, paralyzing it, he sank his teeth into its upper lip.

Unlike the Mexican *charreada,* the American rodeo soon turned into a theatrical business and a very profitable one. When Guy Weadick of Wyoming, a good roper but better showman, organized the Calgary, Alberta, rodeo and offered big prize money to contestants, rodeo riding rapidly became a professional enterprise.

At the same time ranching also changed, becoming

big business, too. Ranches in the Southwest became more and more mechanized until that hallowed American folk hero—the cowboy with his low-slung six-gun and his star-faced mustang—was replaced by ranch hands who are more adept at shifting gears and changing tires than they are at riding or roping a horse.

A real, all-around ranch hand is so scarce now that our federal government has had to set up a school, the Mountain States Ranch School, in Wyoming, to train cowboys. At this school the forty or so students, in addition to studying modern animal husbandry, learn to do things that once came naturally to a cowboy. They are taught how to brand cattle, dehorn calves, and rope steers. They learn how to handle an unbroken bronc in the most surprising way; instead of riding one, they ride a barrel bounced on a suspension cable by their classmates.

In Mexico this situation still has not arisen. Horses are still used on ranches; they do most of the work. *Vaqueros* still brand cattle, dehorn calves, and use the lariat. Even the city riders, the *charros* who specialize in exhibition roping, tailing bulls, riding steers and wild mares, are familiar with the customs and the routine work on ranches. They often contribute their time and skills when work has to be done on shorthanded ranches. In both their work and their play the *charros* maintain the wonderful traditions of the American horse-culture equestrianship.

The question has been asked: Why should anyone interested in horseback riding, even Western-style riding, turn to the Mexican *charro* for pointers? Isn't the *charro's* way of training a horse old-fashioned? Isn't his style of riding too flamboyant and dangerous?

It is true that the *charro's* ideas about horses and horse training are based on a very old tradition, yet experts agree that much of this horse lore is sound. And as for his style of equestrianship being difficult or dangerous, well, we need only turn to the story of Bill Fox.

In 1964 a group of picked Mexican *charros* made a goodwill tour of Europe and Argentina. Among these *charros* who exhibited their horsemanship abroad was a compact, blue-eyed, silver-haired man who rode like a Mexican and spoke like one—but with an American accent. This man was William Fox, a retired U.S. Marine Corps general.

Why a man in his sixties, a man who had been a successful soldier and civil engineer, and who had a California airfield named after him, should take up the spine-twisting *charro* style of riding seems a mystery. To have been included in a group of riders representing Mexico abroad is even more startling. The answer, however, is very simple. Bill Fox, a lean, suntanned, bantam-size man with as much bounce as a coiled spring, found something in Mexico which appealed to his youthful enthusiasm; he found a stallion named Enamorado, and he found the *charreada*.

At the very age that most men want to sit back and take life easy, Bill Fox began riding. He rode with Mexican ranchers and cavalrymen, and he became active in the local *charro* club of the small Mexican town where he had retired. He learned how to tail bulls and to execute the various lasso throws. Although he kept himself in marvelous physical condition, he realized he was not the same man who had flown combat missions in the skies above Guadalcanal twenty years before. There were moments when he despaired of ever learning the things that came so easily to the Mexican *charro*.

In the spring of 1964 word went out from the headquarters of the National Federation of *Charros* that the regional clubs should select two or more riders to become part of the national team that would go abroad on the goodwill tour. Bill Fox took part in the Sunday-morning elimination in his town. He had no expectations of being selected. He knew that a dozen of his teammates were better qualified, and, after all, he had just celebrated his sixty-fifth birthday.

When his turn came up in the *mangana,* he did his best. His rope whirled in a handsome flourish; it sailed out and hooked the flashing legs of the mare running past him. Then suddenly he was in trouble. The harsh istle rope tangled about his wrist and hand. He was jerked head over heels by the running horse. When he finally freed himself, he found that his hand had been badly lacerated, and one finger was almost severed. His companions provided *charro*-style first aid, a liberal dousing of the injured hand with fiery tequila that left him gasping with pain. The club's captain, a magnificent horseman named Javier Orijel, offered to drive him to the hospital.

"I should have let him drive me there," said Bill Fox,

"but for some crazy reason I felt I ought to take my horse."

He rode to the hospital in a semidaze. His hand was treated, stitched up, and the finger was saved. Then, instead of going home, he rode the two miles back to the *charro* ring. He realized that this was not very sensible, yet he felt he ought to be there. He arrived just as the judges and his club mates were finishing a conference. When he entered the ring, he was told that he and Orijel had been selected as the two regional representatives to go to Europe. He would be riding with some of Mexico's most noted *charros,* with Don José Yslas Salazar, with Mariano Pedrero, with Carlos Sánchez, with José Ramos and José Balleza. He was, at last, a true *charro*.

Glossary

ANQUERA — a covering for the hindquarter of the horse.

BAGUALE — the mustang, or wild (feral) horse of Argentina.

BRONCO — a wild or semiwild horse; from the Spanish word meaning rude or rough.

CABRIOLA — from the Spanish, meaning to caper or frisk.

CEJAR — to pace backward smoothly.

CHAPARERAS — leather breeches; chaps.

CHARREADA — the Mexican-style equestrian competition; rodeo.

CHARRO — a Mexican-style rider. The original meaning of the word meant ill-bred, showy, over fancy.

CHORREAR — to let the rope, wound around the saddle horn, slip out smoothly; to dally.

COLA, COLEAR — from the Spanish, meaning tail. *Colear* means to throw an animal by the tail.

ESCARAMUZA — from the Spanish, meaning a skirmish. A horseback drill; a kind of equestrian ballet.

GAMUZA — suede; leather material used for clothing and boots.

HACIENDA — a landed estate.

HONDO — spliced eyelet at the loop end of a rope.

JAQUIMA — a halter; corrupted into hackamore by U.S. cowboys.

JARIPEO — another term for an equestrian contest; a *charreada*.

JINETE — a horseman; from the Berber *Zenete*.

LIENZO — from the Spanish, meaning face or front of a wall. The *lienzo* is the walled-in alleyway section of the *charreada* amphitheater. The ring section of the amphitheater is called the *plaza*.

MACHETE — a long, broad-bladed knife.

MANGANA — a lasso throw catching an animal's front legs. Mexican horsemen refer to the front legs as *manos,* "hands."

MESTENO — mustang; the word is derived from Mesta, a Spanish organization of graziers and herders established in 1537 to regulate the branding of cattle and horses. The Mesta contributed unbranded or wild animals to orphanages.

PASO — a pass or trick.

PEAL — the lasso throw in which the feet (hind legs) of a horse are roped.

RAMAL — romal; a flexible whip made by the bridle reins when they are fastened together.

REATA — rope; lasso.

REJONEAR — to fight a bull on horseback.

VAQUERO — cowboy; from the Spanish *vaca,* "cow." In the American Northwest the word changed into buckaroo.

Index

125

Index

Index

National Federation of *Charros* (Federación Nacional de Charros), 15, 121
Nava, Pedro de, 85
New Mexico, 64, 79–80, 83–84
Nicaragua, 43
Norte, João do, 63–64
North Africa, horses in, 20 ff.
North America, horses in, 17 ff., 24, 35 ff., 61. *See also* specific places, subjects

Oñate, Juan de, 43
Ordáz, Diago de, 35
Orijel, Javier, 121–22

Pampas, 24, 44–45
Parades and reviews, 41–42
Paraguay, 36, 61–62
Patagonia, 18, 48
Peru, 18, 26–27, 36, 42 ff., 63
Pickett, Bill, 118
Pizarro, Francisco, 26 ff., 42
Pommel, 74, 76 ff., 110
Ponce, Father Alonzo, 103
Portolá, Gaspar de, 47
Portuguese horses, 63
Professional riders, 14, 15–16
Pueblo revolts, 46–47
Pueblo saddle, 77

Quarter horse, 71–72, 107
Quixote, Don, 53

Races, 49–50
Ranch show, 117–18
Ranching, 39 ff.
Reata, 109–15
Rodeos, 14, 15–16, 117–18
Rollins, Philip Ashton, 81
Rope twirling, 113–15
Roping, 13–14, 76 ff., 109–15
Rosas, 56

Saddles, 41, 51 ff., 73–80
Salazar, Francisco Cervantes, 64
Sandoval, Gonzalo de, 31
School, ranch hand, 119
Serape, 89
Sidearms, 85
Solanet, Dr. Emilio, 62
South America, horses in, 17 ff., 24, 35 ff., 61 ff. *See also* specific countries, subjects
Southeast, 35
Southwest, 35, 46 ff., 116 ff. *See also* specific places, subjects
Spain, 20, 22 ff., 39, 51 ff.
Spurs, 86
Stirrups, 52 ff., 77

Tapia, Fernando de, 40
Tchiffely, Aime F., 62–63
Texas, 47–48, 77, 110
Thompson, D. W., 80
Thoroughbreds, 20, 49–50
Thorp, Jack, 102
Tour, goodwill, 120–22
Tzimin Chac, 34–35

United States, 9–10, 14 ff. *See also* specific places, subjects

Valdiva, Don Pedro de, 45
Vaqueros, 41, 65
Venezuela, 10, 24, 35, 43, 44, 63
Villar, Don José Alvarez de, 51, 90
Vocabulary, 116–17

Weadick, Guy, 118
Weapons, 26, 41, 85, 111–12
Western saddles, 77–78
"Wild West" shows, 117–18

Young, John Richard, 56, 78
Yucatán, 33–35

Zaldívar, Don Juan, 78
Zaldívar, Vicente, 43–44

127

The Author

JAMES NORMAN, who at present is a faculty lecturer at Ohio University during the winter, has lived in Mexico most of the time since 1950. He has published more than a dozen books and numerous stories and articles in national magazines. While serving as an Army combat correspondent in the Southwest Pacific during World War II, he received a field commission and the Bronze Star.

791.8
NOR

C.2

Norman, James

Charro, Mexican
horseman

$3,49

240 T 11

DATE			
APR 4 1979			
MAR 18 1983